FESTIVALS AND SAINTS DAYS

Trinity Sunday to Advent

by

J. ERNEST RATTENBURY

LONDON : THE EPWORTH PRESS

THE EPWORTH PRESS
(FRANK H. CUMBERS)
25-35 City Road, London, E.C.1

MELBOURNE   CAPE TOWN
NEW YORK   TORONTO

SET IN MONOTYPE BEMBO AND PRINTED IN
GREAT BRITAIN BY THE CAMELOT PRESS LTD.
LONDON AND SOUTHAMPTON

FESTIVALS AND SAINTS DAYS

TO

COLONEL AND MRS CECIL THOMPSON

OF NUNWICK HALL

with many thanks for much kindness

PREFACE

I HAVE published in recent years three volumes of devotional studies based on the Gospels, Epistles and Collects of the Sundays of the Christian year: *The Throne, the Cradle, and the Star*, deals with the Sundays between Advent and Lent; *The Adoration of the Lamb* with those between Lent and Easter; and *O'er Every Foe Victorious* with those between Easter and Trinity Sunday. In addition, in two booklets, I have dealt with *The Seven Words of Jesus on the Cross* and in *The Spirit and the Bride* with the last words of our Saviour to His Apostles.

Some of my correspondents remind me that I have said nothing about the twenty-five Sundays after Trinity, and have asked me to do so. It is quite true, of course, that I have not written on the Gospels and Epistles of these Sundays for the reason that in some sense the Christian year begins with Advent and ends with Trinity Sunday. These are the days which deal with the historical events of Our Lord's life, death, resurrection, and ascension, and of the affusion of the Holy Ghost, culminating with the day devoted to the Holy Trinity—the fundamental truth of Christian Doctrine. The Sundays between Trinity and Advent are not based on historical facts, and lack continuity of thought. Whilst a study of the Gospels and Epistles of these days is undoubtedly profitable, they are without the actual basis which underlies my devotional writings. I am limited, too, by space and time.

My publishers will afford me small space in these days, and in my eighty-fifth year, I naturally want to make the best of the days that are left to me.

The problem that I have to solve is whether I can write profitably of the interval between Trinity Sunday and Advent. I think and hope that I may be able to do so. Factual treatment seems to me possible by means of Meditation upon the Festival Days which the Prayer Book authorizes for our observance. Of these there are six in this period. They are Lammas Day the Transfiguration, The Name of Jesus, Holy Cross, Michael-mas, and All Saints' Day. To these I propose to add a study of the twenty-third Sunday after Trinity, which falls between the 4th Sundays in October and November—the Sunday which begins Christian Citizenship week, to which a special attention is called by the Conference of my Church. It may be coincidence that the Gospel and Epistle of that day are peculiarly appropriate to consideration of civic obligations.

Including the introductory chapter, these will supply us with seven studies of the twelve which I can make.

In the Second Prayer Book of King Edward the Sixth an explanation of the rejection and adoption of certain ancient ceremonies was written under the title: 'Of Ceremonies, why some be abolished, and some retained.' The ceremonies retained therefore were the result of careful thought and examination. In the period of the Christian year of which we are thinking, thirty-eight Saints' days are retained for observation: of these, seven are the days of Apostles and other New Testament characters for which the Gospels, Epistles and Collects are employed and their observance is enjoined upon the Church. These festivals of thanksgiving are for St James, St Simon and St Jude, St Peter, St Matthew, St John the Baptist, St Luke, and St Bartholomew. But though these days might well be the subjects of devotional studies, I cannot deal with them because in the present series of books, I have already dealt with St Peter,[1] St John the Baptist,[2] and St Jude[3]. Also I have published sermons on St James, St Matthew, and St Bartholomew. Hence I shall deal only here with St Luke the Evangelist and St Bartholomew, the latter from a different stand-point from that in which he was treated in my earlier book.

From the other Saints commemorated in this period, I choose, rather arbitrarily, St Mary Magdalen, whose day was celebrated in the First Prayer Book of King Edward the Sixth, with Gospel

[1] See *Adoration of the Lamb* and *O'er Every Foe Victorious.*
[2] See *The Throne, the Cradle, and the Star.*
[3] See *The Spirit and the Bride.*

and Epistle; for some unaccountable reason the Gospel and Epistle are omitted in the present Prayer Book. My other choice is St Hugh of Lincoln, a great medieval Saint whose memory should be kept green.

The underlying fact of all festival days is the obligation of gratitude to God and the truth of the vital presence of our Saviour amongst his people. The early Christians were a grateful people. They named their great festival 'Eucharist' which in English simply means Thanksgiving. Gratitude to God is a primary Christian feature. Someone once said: 'Everybody can say, "God help me!"—but only Christians can truly say, "We thank thee Oh God!"' This statement may not be more than a half-truth, but it has a significance worthy of thought.

In an American book about prayer the author said that to a modern American thanksgiving was the greatest difficulty, because Americans had the habit of paying for everything that they received; and the sense of gratitude, even to God, was an embarrassment to them. I am sure that many Americans would not agree with this statement, but the sense of personal efficiency may tend to undermine the humility which expresses itself in gratitude. Can there be any sin more deplorable than the sin of ingratitude? The joyous gratitude of the early Church sets before us an example never to be forgotten, and the value of special days of praise and thanksgiving cannot be over-estimated when we remember some of the blessings we have received from God. These are the days on which we are most emphatically called to say:

> *Bless the Lord, O my soul;*
> *And all that is within me, bless his holy name.*
> *Bless the Lord, O my soul,*
> *And forget not all his benefits.*

CONTENTS

NOTE

I express my thanks to my brother, the Rev. Harold Rattenbury, for his helpful reading of my typescript, and his valuable suggestions; and to Miss Marjorie Harry for her careful reading and correction of the proofs.

J. E. R.

CHAPTER ONE

INTRODUCTION

RELICS AND FESTIVALS

We praise Thee, O God; we acknowledge Thee to be the Lord.
All the earth doth worship Thee, the Father everlasting.
To Thee all Angels cry aloud, the Heavens and all the Powers therein;
To thee Cherubin and Seraphin continually do cry;
Holy, Holy, Holy; Lord God of Sabaoth;
Heaven and earth are full of the Majesty of Thy Glory.
The glorious company of the Apostles praise Thee;
The noble army of Martyrs praise Thee;
The holy Church throughout all the world doth acknowledge Thee—
The Father of an Infinite Majesty.

WHAT is the origin of the feasts and festivals of the Church? In the first two or three centuries of Christianity there were only, as Dom Gregory Dix points out, two annual feasts: the Easter-Paschal and the Whitsuntide Feasts. There was also a weekly festival of thanksgiving for Easter Sunday. This was not the Jewish Sabbath—a day which the Gentile Christians did not observe. It may of course be true that the weekly Sabbath of the Jews influenced the Christian weekly celebrations; but so far as the Sunday is related to the Fourth Commandment, it celebrated not the resting from the Creation of the world as expressed in the Exodus account of the Commandments, but rather the liberation of the Israelites from Egypt as expressed in Deuteronomy. The weekly Eucharist was of course a weekly thanksgiving for Easter.

How then was it that in later centuries the festivals of the Church originated? There can be little doubt that the source of these festivals is to be found in the veneration of the martyrs. The heroic witness that these men and women bore to Christ was a living evidence of His presence amongst His people: the greatest evidence of Christianity is always the Christian, that is to say, it is the man who makes Christianity evident.

Although in the Acts of the Apostles we have the account of the martyrdom of St Stephen and information about that of St James, it is in the Book of Revelation, written, as it was, in a time of acute persecution, that we first became acquainted with the reverence with which the martyrs were held: 'And when he had opened the fifth seal, I saw under the altar the souls of them that were slain for the word of God, and for the testimony which they held: and they cried with a loud voice, saying, How long, O Lord. . . .' And then in Chapter 7 we read: 'What are these which are arrayed in white robes? and whence came they? And I said unto him, Sir, thou knowest. And he said to me, These are they which came out of great tribulation, and have washed their robes, and made them white in the blood of the Lamb.'

The first authentic account that we have of a martyr of the post apostolic Church is the vivid description of the death of St Polycarp.[1] The story is beautifully told by a witness of the death (in A.D. 155) of this venerable Bishop of Smyrna who then challenged by the Roman Pro-Consul to deny Christ, courageously said: 'For eighty-and-six years have I been His servant, and He has done me no wrong, and how can I blaspheme my King who saved me?' But when the Pro-Consul persisted again, and said: 'Swear by the genius of Cæsar,' he answered him: 'If you vainly suppose that I will swear by the genius of Cæsar, as you say, and pretend that you are ignorant who I am, listen plainly: I am a Christian. . . .' Already he had heard a voice which others heard as well saying: 'Be strong, Polycarp, and play the man.' Never was the man more nobly played than by this aged Saint. First of all the Roman authority threatened him with wild beasts, but because for some reason he seemed disdainful of the beasts, the Pro-Consul said that he should be burnt to death. The excited and hostile crowd quickly collected faggots and Polycarp was sent in the midst of them. When the fire was ignited, for some reason, the Christians presumably thought by a supernatural intervention, the fire surrounded but did not burn

[1] See Kirsopp Lake, *Apostolic Fathers*, II.313.

him. In time, of course, he would have died through the heat, but his persecutors were impatient and a soldier stabbed him with a dagger. The Christians were anxious to get his body in order to have 'communion with his flesh', but to prevent this, he was thrown upon the fire and his body was burnt. The Christians contented themselves with collecting what bones of him were left, which they said were 'more precious than precious stones, and finer than gold' and 'put them where it was meet'. 'There' they said, 'the Lord will permit us to come together according to our power in gladness and joy, and celebrate the birthday of his martyrdom, both in memory of those who have already contested, and for the practice and training of those whose fate it shall be.'

St Polycarp was a great man of outstanding personality, but though there were renegades, men who denied Christ and saved their lives, martyrs for their faith were numerous and brave men and women were venerated in many villages and towns. They were canonized, not by ecclesiastical authority, but by local sentiment. In many places the day of their birth or martyrdom was celebrated. And so the local Saints' Days gradually developed. By analogy other festivals commemorating great Christian events or truths also came to be celebrated: the Feast of Christmas being the most conspicuous.

One noticeable fact about the martyrdom of Polycarp is the valuation that the story puts upon his relics. They were more precious than gems or silver or gold. In time to come, though this would not be true then, relics had so great a value that men fought for their possession. The spiritual value of Saints' Days and Festival Days is seen in the fact that they are vital expressions of Christian gratitude to God for His gifts. There are no gifts greater than good men and women. They also demonstrate the fact that Christ is not dead, but living in His Living Body, the Holy Church. But there were also values not altogether spiritual —the relics.

To most Protestants, the reverence of relics seems to be an unfortunate distortion in the veneration of Saints and martyrs.

It is important, however, that we should try to understand the mentality and the philosophy, crude though it may be, of people of other ages. The veneration of relics is not a Catholic or even a Christian invention. There is a deep human characteristic of which all are aware, lying beneath it. We all cherish keepsakes, mementoes, portraits of those who are dear to us and have left us, and this of course is fundamental in relic veneration. But to get back to the thoughts of early people, we must begin with the living. We have all come across personalities so radiant in their influence that their presence brightens any company they are in. This is true of very vital people and is particularly true of (in the most comprehensive sense of the word) the Saints. In ancient times a theory seems to have been formed that such people emitted a radiance which left its impression even on material things, and when they died, their relics were cherished. The valuation of them was enhanced by the fact that for Christians their departed were not dead, but living, and their material relics, not only their bones, but the garments which had been in contact with their wearers were permanently enriched by their contact. The explanation of what seems to us superstition, is to be found in the philosophy of the time.

The popular feeling, though this was by no means confined to the populace, was that an efflux flowed from outstanding personalities to everything with which they were in contact. Not only did contact-matter, but also portraits or shadows were regarded in some sense as part of the personality of the person shadowed or portrayed. Magicians, who worked, it is true, through hate and not through love, would mutilate the portrait of an enemy and think that they had done damage to the man himself. This sense of the importance of contact and of imitation is to be found even in Holy Scripture: 'And by the hands of the apostles were many signs and wonders wrought among the people; . . . insomuch that they brought forth the sick into the streets, and laid them on beds and couches, that at the least the shadow of Peter passing by might overshadow some of them.'[2] 'And God wrought special miracles by the hands of Paul: So that from his body were brought unto the sick handkerchiefs or aprons, and the diseases departed from them, and the evil spirits went out of them.'[3] It is evident from these passages that in a sense the shadow of Peter was thought to be Peter and the handkerchiefs which had touched Paul were the recipients, as it were, of an efflux of his personality, which gave them healing power. While the Scriptures can hardly be said to commend such views, they certainly do not condemn them, and it is easy to see that the relics of an outstanding personality would not lose through the death of that personality the power that contact had given to them.

We must never forget that people of earlier ages were naturally influenced both by the cosmology and psychology of their times, though these may be as unintelligible to us as eons and protons would have been to them.[4]

Modern Catholics not only admit, but affirm, that great abuses arose from the belief in the miracle-working power of relics.[5] One of these abuses was the manufacture of false relics. This was sometimes actually defended on the theory of imitation. Some relic or portrait was copied and brought into contact with the genuine relic, and thus it was thought that the efflux of the genuine was communicated to its copy, on the principle of 'imitation'. It must not be forgotten, however, that the greatest Fathers of the Church realized the danger of the multiplication of relics. St Augustine, especially, denounced the manufacture as roguery. Relics indeed had an economic value. They were more precious than gold or silver to men who traded in them, and a very brisk trade was carried on, especially in medieval times, in manufactured relics. It is difficult for us today to understand the mentality of those, particularly of medieval times, who expected miracles. When one reads that entrancing book by the Venerable Bede, *The Ecclesiastical History of England*,

---

[2] Acts 5¹².   [3] Acts 19¹¹.
[4] For an objective account of relics, see Irjo Hirn, *The Sacred Shrine*.
[5] See *Catholic Encyclopedia*.

or his *Life of St Cuthbert*, his belief in miracles and his explanation of phenomena and fact which to us are so obviously explained by natural causes is very surprising. Indeed, one can almost sympathize with the attitude of Denys in Charles Reade's *The Cloister and the Hearth*. When he came into contact with excited people and asked what had happened, he was informed a miracle. His interest vanished as he said 'Only a miracle', as if miracles were too-common occurrences to be especially notable. Perhaps we in our time have lost this sense of wonder that our ancestors had, and it is no easy thing for the children of one age to understand those of another. We tend to explain everything, even the inexplicable, by natural causes. They seemed to give hypernatural explanations for anything even slightly unusual. The traffic in relics and the worship of the relics was always regarded by the Church with caution. When speaking of reverence for the Saints, the authorities emphasized that worship was to God alone. There were ecclesiastics who greatly discussed the cult of the reliquary; a conspicuous instance of a Saint's contempt for the emphasis on relics is to be found in the story related of St Hugh of Lincoln on page ooo, *infra*.

Harnack[6] asserts that the reverence given to the Saints in the middle ages was almost entirely due to the belief in their intercession. The need for the intercession of the Saints is a difficulty to the modern Protestant, who feels that there lives One in Heaven who ever lives to make intercession for us.[7] As St Paul says, 'We have in Christ free access to God', and the Epistle to the Hebrews exhorts us to Come boldly unto the throne of grace. We are to come to One who, because He is 'touched with the feeling of our infirmity', 'being tempted in all points like as we are', freely offers His help to all who need it. While it is quite true that Christian people on earth pray for each other and that their prayers of love are acceptable, it does seem strange to a Protestant that where such free access to Christ Himself is offered, intermediaries in Heaven should be regarded as necessary. This, as Chapter 10 shows, must not be taken to imply that

[6] See *History of Dogma*, IV.III.   [7] Romans 8[34].

there is no such thing as Communion of Christians on earth with the Saints in Heaven. Now that they are in heaven, those who loved us and prayed for us on earth cannot be indifferent to our needs.

The prayers in the greatest books of Catholic devotion (St Augustine's *Confessions*, Thomas à Kempis's *Imitation of Christ*, and a cycle of verses such as *Dulcis Memoria*) are invariably addressed to God Himself or to our Saviour and not to the Saints; and yet nothing can be more profitable than reverence to the memories of the great spiritual heroes of the world. Few people, whether Catholic or Protestant, today would fail to accept the words of St Jerome: 'We do not worship, and we do not adore for fear we should bow down to the creature rather than to the Creator, but we venerate the relics of the martyrs in order to adore Him whose martyrs and witness they were.'

At the time of the Reformation, nothing shocked and scandalized the Reformers more than the current abuses of relic and Saint worship. The remarkable and well-known account which Erasmus gave of a pilgrimage which he and Dean Colet made to the shrine of Thomas à Becket at Canterbury, shows the contempt and scorn with which he and his friends regarded both the superstitions and the unscrupulous use made of relics. Sir Thomas More, recently canonized by the Church of Rome, their intimate friend and companion, did not join them in their pilgrimage but almost certainly agreed with their sentiment. Indeed the Council of Trent itself, while it sanctioned the veneration of relics, was most careful to warn people of the dangers of superstition.

Enthusiastic reformers, when they pluck up tares, are always in danger of plucking up the wheat as well. While the abuses of relic worship as most modern Christians, whether Catholic or Protestant, would agree, needed stern treatment, it was equally true that the veneration of the Saints is a practice to be encouraged when its abuses are removed. One of the results, especially amongst the Puritans, of reforming zeal was to abolish all festivals and Saints' days. In Scotland, for instance, even Christmas festivities were done away with, because there is no mention in the New Testament of yule logs and Christmas trees. Surely the command of Gregory the Great to St Augustine of Canterbury, not to abolish heathen festivals, but to substitute for them some Christian solemnity, and so, as it were, to baptize them into Christ, was the better method.

We must give thanks to God for innumerable mercies, but for none more than good men and women. The words that Robert Browning puts into the mouth of a Pope about a good woman, should never be forgotten:

> *Through such souls alone*
> *God stooping shows sufficient of His light*
> *For us i' the dark to rise by.*

The Anglican calendar clearly demonstrates that while a number of Saints' days and Festivals were removed for the reason given in the statement on Ceremonies in the Second Prayer Book of King Edward the Sixth, many remain. It is true that some of these are of little more than antiquarian interest to modern men. St Swithin, for instance, may be discussed by weather prophets, but hardly excites devotion or rapture. Quite a number of the Saints whose days are still quoted in the Anglican calendar have long since become almost meaningless names to modern Englishmen. It is notable, too, in this calendar, that the most recent Saint whose day is celebrated died more than 700 years ago—St Hugh of Lincoln. Is it really credible that no Saints have lived or should be venerated in the last 700 years? One wonders whether, if the Christian calendar could have been composed with foresight, the Sundays between Trinity and Advent could not have been devoted to the commemoration of martyrs and Saints who through the long centuries have been true witnesses of the presence of the Living Christ amongst His people. The Christian year from Advent to Trinity commemorates and brings to life the Gospel story, but Christ is not dead; He lives. 'Jesus Christ is the same yesterday, today and for ever,' and had it been possible, it might have been a good thing to fill up gradually festivals and commemorations of His continuing activities. In the nature of things such a scheme was not possible, and other motives have commanded the construction of the calendar as it exists. Yet one could wish that there were some way of cherishing the memory of men like Bishop Andrewes, Bishop Ken, Bishop King, George Herbert, to say nothing of the Saints of the Evangelical revival. The Anglican Church of course lacks any method of canonization, and its one attempt to commemorate a martyr was very unfortunate. Charles the First can hardly be called a Saint, and the satirical remark of Maximin Piette in his admirable biography of John Wesley, that the only distinctive doctrine that the Anglican church has formulated is that of the Divine Right of Kings, is, though a witticism, not without point.

Is there a better way of commemorating the Saints of the Church and thus of exemplifying the continual presence of Christ among his people than that of Festival and Saints days? No one realized better the value of good men to Christian people than John Wesley. His favourite festival was that of All Saints, which he observed by celebrations of Holy Communion throughout the Octave. His pursuit of holiness and his fervent wish that his people should pursue it made him a diligent student of the lives of the Saints of all ages. His references to these men are extraordinarily eclectic. He recognized the holy life in his contemporaries, whatever their denomination. The life of a Catholic, M. De Ranty, and even of a Socinian, Firmin, are both recommended to his people as models of sanctity. Modern Methodists give little attention to the Saints, but a recent and important exception is to be found in the remarkable book of Dr W. E. Sangster, *The Pure in Heart*. This book, which gives a succinct account of Roman and Greek methods of canonization, deals with the lives of Saints, particularly modern ones, both Catholic and Protestant. He finds models of a holy life in men like the Curé d'Ars and David Hill, a great Methodist missionary whose witness to Christ in China should never be forgotten.

All seekers for the holy life need the help in modern times of modern witnesses to Christ. Men and women who manifest the power and presence of Christ by their holy lives are of infinitely more value to seekers of holiness than the exhortation and doctrine of theorists however excellent. We cannot but be thankful for the testimonies of the Saints of every age; but the testimony of men who have overcome the difficulties which beset us all today obviously have a special value for us.

Sometimes, I have played with the idea, which I cannot, I fear, put into effect, of suggesting a new use of the Christian calendar. Would it be possible to read carefully the Collects, Epistles and Gospels of the Sundays between Trinity and Advent, and to find in the life of some Saint of the later centuries an example which would illustrate them. Whenever I have casually opened the Prayer Book at a particular day, some Saint has come to my mind as an illustration of the teaching of that day—in one case St Vincent de Paul, in another, Silas Told. So one might go on, and in this way give a factual illustration of these weekly devotions. I think this would be a profitable way of treating Gospels and Epistles which do seem rather to hang in the air and lack, as I have said, a factual basis and continuity. This, however, is beyond my power, but I commend the method to others who have a knowledge of the Saints.

In the last few centuries many Saints have been added to the lists of devout men and women to be venerated by Christian people. There are great Saints of the Catholic Church whose names are venerated by Protestants, and that the Church of Rome still produces Saints is a fact that all Protestants should remember and reflect upon. Nevertheless, one cannot but wish that the holy people of a different faith might be commemorated. Methodists have one Saint's day, 24th May, when they commemorate the Conversion of John Wesley. Thank God there are many names that might be added to his. Joseph Boswell records that when he visited Voltaire, he asked that great mocker whether he had ever seen a Saint, and Voltaire replied without comment, 'I once met John Fletcher', and I do not think he was speaking in mockery. In recent years, no more saintly man than the Methodist John Fletcher of Madeley has lived. Wesley was careful to obtain from his preachers accounts of their spiritual life, and the six volumes of the lives of the early Methodist preachers, still remain, however little read, an extraordinary record of devoted saintly lives. A man like Thomas Walsh for instance, would undoubtedly have been canonized if he had remained a Roman Catholic, because some events in his life would have complied with the Roman rule that a Saint must have at least two miracles to his credit. In a word, may I say that the veneration of the Saints remains a duty and privilege of Christian people which cannot be dismissed because in some times and places it has been mingled with superstition.

CHAPTER TWO

ST MARY MAGDALEN

(22nd July)

Epistle: Wisdom 3². *Gospel:* Luke 7³⁶.

> *Like Mary's gift, may my devotion prove,*
> *Forgiven greatly, how I greatly love.*

FOR the Gospel and Epistle for St Mary Magdalen's Day, we must go to the first Prayer Book of King Edward the Sixth. The Gospel of the Day is Luke 7³⁶⁻⁵⁰, the story of the woman of the city who in Simon the Pharisee's house washed the feet of our Saviour with her tears and wiped them with the hair of her head and anointed His feet with ointment. The fact that this incident is recorded on the day of St Mary Magdalen proves that the authorities of the Church identified the Magdalen with the woman of the city. In our own day this identification has often been questioned, as also has the traditional identification of Mary Magdalen with Mary of Bethany. Some commentators argue that there are three separate women described here; others that there are two; but the tradition of the western Church that the three were identical has never really been disproved. One favourite argument, that the moral difference between Mary of Bethany and the woman of the city is so great that it is impossible to identify them, is I am sure unsound, and, consciously or unconsciously, springs from a disbelief of the power of Jesus, not only to forgive sins, but to transform sinners. He who forgives the sinner 'breaks the power of cancelled sin', as Charles Wesley wrote.

While I incline to accept the ancient tradition, positive demonstration in such a case seems to be quite impossible. As the relation of Mary of Bethany to Mary Magdalen is irrelevant in the study of this chapter, I will not discuss the question, but will assume the identification of the woman who was a sinner with Mary Magdalen out of whom our Lord cast seven devils.

There are one or two preliminary questions that must be asked and answered. Was the woman's love the result or the cause of her pardon? In our version it would seem that it was the cause—'Her sins, which are many, are forgiven; for she loved much'; but the parable of the two debtors hardly seems to make sense, unless the love is the result of the pardon which she received. Jesus compares two people, one with small obligations to his creditor and the other with great, and exacts from the Pharisee the opinion that the love of the one who is forgiven the greater debt will be in excess of the one who is forgiven for a trifling debt. The problem I think has been cleared by the translation of this text by Dr Torrey, the great Aramaic scholar, who has retranslated the Greek text into the original Aramaic words which were actually spoken. He says the result is that these words should be translated: 'She whose many sins were forgiven, loved much.'

The second question is: 'Did this woman come into this Pharisee's house as a penitent, as it is often assumed, asking for forgiveness?' This assumption I think is quite wrong. The woman was a sinner who had been forgiven, and she came into the house of the Pharisee with her thank-offering of love for the pardon which she had received. The hymn which we so often sing, quite rightly prays:

> *Like Mary's gift, may my devotion prove,*
> *Forgiven greatly, how I greatly love.*

Our Lord accepted her gift and confirmed His pardon of her sins and told her: 'Thy faith hath saved thee.'

St Luke's graphic power of constructing word pictures is illustrated better in none of his writings than in the story of the woman who was a sinner. How easily we picture the reclining figure of our Lord with a weeping woman at His feet, so tenderly and carefully washing them with her tears and kissing them. The Lord Himself though accepting her loving gift of ointment speaks no word of reproach to this woman, notorious as she seems to have been. And the frowning Pharisee stands there, not I think an ignoble figure, but a puzzled man, shocked by what seems to him a scandalous action. We see, too, the face of the other pharisees evidently sharing the opinions of their host and muttering their criticisms.

Perhaps we can best appreciate the significance of the scene by practising a little thought-reading. What was the Pharisee thinking? What was the Saviour thinking? What was the woman thinking?

The Pharisee's thoughts are explicitly stated; probably he had heard Jesus talking and had been impressed by the words He spoke, and may well have wondered whether the Pharisees were not too harsh in their judgements on this remarkable man. He at least was grateful to the Prophet whose illuminating words had impressed him, and he had invited Him to his house to dine, possibly congratulating himself on his liberality of thought. But now as he looks at this woman, a well-known person in his city, who was condemned by the decent people of the time, he begins to wonder whether he has done well. She was a sinner. And yet this Man whom everybody thought a Prophet, permitted her to kiss His feet. He gave her no good advice, no reproach fell from His lips. Could He be a Prophet? Elijah came to his mind. Is this the way in which Elijah, whose treatment of Jezebel he called to mind, would have treated this notorious woman? Was this Man really a prophet or a charlatan? Prophets in the Old Testament are called seers, could a prophet be beguiled by the trickeries of this evil person? She was a sinner; the right way to treat such sinners in accordance with the Jewish Law was to stone them. The attitude of respectable persons in all generations to such women has been to tie them to the cart tail and whip them round the streets. How could morality be sustained if such people were tolerated, and even in this case encouraged? Was the Man a prophet? Certainly to the mind of the Pharisee he was no seer.

What was Jesus thinking? The Pharisee's thoughts are obvious: the woman is a sinner. Our Lord's thoughts are obvious too: the sinner is a woman—a woman made in the image of God. Jesus was conscious enough of her sin, but He saw through it and behind it. The Pharisee saw the sin; but 'the eyes of Him who beholdeth not evil' saw through the sin to a daughter of the Living God. Love can see what criticism will never see.

Some years ago, I met weekly a class of newly converted men. Most of them were educated men, but one was a notorious loud-voiced atheist, well known at the time in the city of Nottingham. I had great joy in watching the development in the knowledge of God of this man who had been His violent opponent. One evening I spoke to him about the meeting that we had held on the previous Friday night, and asked him whether he enjoyed it. 'Yes,' he said, 'but I enjoyed something more afterwards.' The class had gone on to a late hour the week before, and he told me how he and his friend had to walk home in a stormy night, which did not suggest to me any great enjoyment. It was time for the closing of public-houses. 'As I was passing one with which I was familiar, a drunken man was literally thrown out of the house into the street, and rolled over into the gutter. We knew the man and my friend said: "We had better take him home." I replied: "No, leave the beast there, the gutter is his home." "No," my friend said, "we'll take him home." So I took hold of one arm and he took hold of the other, and we dragged him out of the gutter, the rain pelting on us all the time; but he struggled with us, with the consequence that I fell on top of him into the gutter. I got up and said angrily: "Let the beast stay where he is." But my friend persisted, and so we dragged him along to his home a few hundred yards away. We opened the door and flung him into the passage; when suddenly we heard the clattering of little feet upon the stairs, and a little girl came down saying, "Daddy, daddy, I am glad you've come home. I knew I could keep awake until you came," and kissed him.'

'Well,' I said, 'what did you learn from that?'

'I learnt,' he replied, 'that love could see a father where I could only see a beast.'

This is just what happened in the Pharisee's house. Critical eyes could see only a sinner; but the loving eyes of Jesus saw a woman, saw in her that angel of the little one and of the lost sheep which is always before the face of God.

But what did Jesus think about the Pharisee? The Pharisee was His host, and he treated Him courteously. The parable of the two debtors which He spoke to him was an acknowledgement that although the Pharisee was indebted to Him, the debt was a relatively small one, and by his invitation to Jesus he had cancelled it. Though the Lord reminded him that his welcome was rather a cold one, and that he did not treat Him with the hospitality which would be given to an honoured guest, yet He agreed that Simon had acknowledged his obligation. The poor woman's more generous gift of ointment and effusive love was a natural expression of gratitude for her liberation from the seven devils with which she was possessed. She loved much because she had been forgiven much.

In a much quoted saying, Montefiori censures Jesus for his harsh treatment of the Pharisees; but it must not be forgotten that Jesus did not fail in love to the Pharisees, and that the only way in which their self-complacency could be shattered was by the whip with which He scourged them. I do not think our Lord was without sympathy with them. It is true, as Niebuhr says, that they were the best people of the day in which Christ lived; they obeyed the law according to their light, and they stood as no other people did, for morality.

Many years ago, I heard an eminent preacher compare the religious denominations of his day with the various sects of the time of our Lord. The Anglicans, he said, were the Sadducees of that time; the political non-conformists, the Herodians; and the Methodists, the Pharisees. I was not pleased at the moment as a Methodist, to be numbered among the Pharisees; but reflection suggested to me that his description had about as much truth in it as other generalizations of this sort have.

Two hundred years before, the fathers of the Pharisees were a noble group of men who by their fidelity and courage maintained the truth of God in degenerate days. In our Lord's day they were a respectable community, but lacked the fervour of their ancestors. I could not help wondering whether the very respectable community of the Methodist people of my own time had not suffered a like degeneration. Had not many of them lost their first love. Could they sing fervently as Charles Wesley sang, in his conversion:

> *. . . on you I call,*
> *Harlots, and publicans, . . .*

I remember well sitting in my study one day after reading again this narrative, asking myself: 'What would you have done, if you had been in the Pharisee's house and had seen what the Pharisee saw?' I know too well, through years of experience of rescue work of fallen women, the corruption and foulness of their lives. Ought a Christian man to tolerate such people? I tried to picture what would happen if a woman of this sort came into a gathering of respectable Methodist women who had met together to sew for some charitable cause. I cannot think that she would be very welcome. As I thought about this whole incident, I could not help feeling that if I had never read the story in St Luke's gospel, my sympathies might well have been with the Pharisee rather than with the Saviour. But then of course we have read the incident and it makes a difference. And yet I remember how once I was appalled by the Phariseeism of some of my fellow Methodists. It was many years ago, when I conducted for the first time in my life an evangelical Mission in an English village. The services in some ways had been disappointing to me, but one day I heard that there was a man in the village who had killed another man in a drunken brawl. In a few days he was to appear at the Assizes charged either with murder or manslaughter, and I was told that he was in a strange state of misery, so I went to his house to visit him. His distress was terrible. I found that he was entirely ignorant of religion, but I besought him to turn to Christ, and ask for forgiveness. He did not know what I meant. I asked him to pray, but he said that he had forgotten how and did not even remember the Lord's Prayer; however, I assured him of the forgiveness that God gave to penitent people, and knelt down and prayed with him. And then I witnessed a miracle. The man stood up and with radiant though tearful face, and said that he knew that God had forgiven his sins. I can never forget the almost intoxicating sense of rapture and joy that there was in that man's face and voice. I was quite certain that something had happened suddenly, and as I think miraculously, to change that man. It was on a Friday evening, and I said: 'Of course you will come to the Chapel on Sunday morning to service now.' And he replied: 'Yes I will come.' With all the enthusiasm of youth, I resolved to call on two ladies, the pillars of the little church, women of wealth and position in the village, and ask them when he came to say a word of welcome and encouragement. When I entered the house, I said: 'Have you heard the news?' 'What news?' they said. 'William—has been converted.'

'What nonsense,' they said, 'he will be in prison in a few weeks' time; how can such a man be converted?'

'I am quite sure,' I said, 'that the poor fellow is an entirely changed man, and I have come to ask you next Sunday morning to shake hands with him and give him a welcome to the chapel.'

I can never forget their response: 'Shake hands with a man like that! We are respectable people. Do you really think we can demean ourselves in such a way? We will do nothing of the sort.'

I was very young at the time, and perhaps rather intemperately I talked to them about the elder brother in the parable of the Prodigal Son; but bad as an elder brother is, an elder sister seems to be rather worse!

The man had to serve a sentence of imprisonment for manslaughter, but after all the trials and persecutions he underwent, he remained a Christian man, and actually in a relatively short time became the Sunday-school superintentent at that chapel.

'Alas for the rarity of Christian charity under the sun!'

I believed then, and believe now, that the Methodist people

are a respectable and God-fearing community; but I would we had that passionate love of our Saviour for the souls of men which expressed itself with such enthusiasm in the early Methodists both in word and action as they sang the memorable words: 'O let me commend my Saviour to you.'

But what did the woman think? Not of the Pharisee. He mattered nothing. All her thoughts and love were concentrated upon her Saviour. This poor woman had been treated badly by bad men, and contemptuously by good ones; but now she had met a man of supreme goodness, who did not pass her by on the other side of the street, but cast out of her seven devils—the first good man she ever met who respected her and believed in her, who saw what she really was, and saw through the evil things that were apparent to others. No doubt she would fear sometimes the return of the seven devils, but in His companionship she had no fear. If there is truth in the various legends of Mary Magdalen, she followed Him with the fidelity of a dog. When the women are mentioned who followed Jesus, special notice is made by the Evangelist of Mary Magdalen. We rightly think of the sorrows of the Mother of our Lord at Calvary, but what of this woman's sorrows when He died? The one person on whom she relied for help was gone—what if those seven devils returned again? in the blackness of Calvary her lodestar was blotted out of the sky. Her sorrow and grief must have been desperate. What could she do? All that remained to her was to feed her heart and imagination with memories of Jesus, and so she was first at the tomb to bring her offerings of love; but when the tomb was empty and she met the gardener, no deeper cry of despair ever clove the air than the anguished cry of Mary Magdalen: 'They have taken away my Lord and I know not where they have laid Him.' How indescribable must have been her joy when a familiar voice said 'Mary', and she replied, 'Rabboni!'

Years ago, I remember reading a letter in a well-known weekly journal from a man who was a lover of birds. One day he saw a crippled sparrow on his lawn, and he set its wing and

c

put it into a cage. In the same room there was a canary, a great songster. He said that after a time the chirping sparrow seemed to be changing its note and to be trying, however imperfectly, to sing like the canary. But the canary died and the sparrow, after a few days, died too. Mary, in the companionship of Jesus, learnt to be like Him. The difference between her and Him was as great as that between the sparrow's and the canary's song; but if Jesus died, Mary would die too; she felt herself that she would fail. But He rose again, and Mary knew, as all Christians know, that He lives. And in companionship with Him in His risen life, she conquered until she entered into His immediate presence.

The Church does well to keep in mind this woman who greatly sinned and was greatly forgiven. In few incidents in the Scriptures can we better realize the immeasurable love of a pardoned God.

> *Through the sinful woman shriven,*
> *Through the dying thief forgiven,*
> *Thou to me a hope hast given.*

CHAPTER THREE

LAMMAS DAY

(1st August; 7th Sunday after Trinity [1954])
Epistle: Romans 6¹⁹. *Gospel:* Mark 8¹.

> *For my life and clothes and food*
> *And every comfort here*
> *Thee my most indulgent God*
> *I thank with heart sincere*
> *For Thy blessings numberless—*
>
> *Bless the Lord, O my soul,*
> *And forget not all His benefits.*
>
> *Praise, O praise our God and King!*
> *Hymns of adoration sing:*
>
> *Praise Him for our harvest store,*
> *He hath filled the garner floor:*
>
> *And for richer food than this,*
> *Pledge of everlasting bliss:*
>
> > *For His mercies still endure,*
> > *Ever faithful, ever sure.*

THE Festival of Lammas Day, though authorized in the Anglican calendar, is one to which little, if any, observance seems to be given. The day indeed has rather become a date—1st August—than a Christian festival. It is the name of a day on which rents fall due in some cases and are paid! Readers of Shakespeare will remember how the Nurse refers to it as the birthday of Juliet. What religious significance has it? If you turn to the Gospel and Epistle of Lammas Day, you will find they are all about Peter. The Gospel quotes the famous words, 'Thou art Peter, and upon this rock I will build my Church' (Matt 16¹⁸), and the Epistle is the account in the Acts of the Apostles of Peter's imprisonment under Herod (Acts 12¹). But what has St Peter to do with Lammas Day?

The Catholic commemoration of St Peter's Chains became connected with Lammas Day by chance. The delivery of St

Peter from prison took place in the Spring soon after Passover; but it happened that the Church of St Peter ad Vincula, which was to enshrine the sacred relics, his fetters, was built and dedicated on Lammas Day and the commemoration of the date became popular.

Lammas Day has become a day devoted to St Peter. It is just the name of St Peter's day. But has it no significance in its own right?

In the Middle Ages, when people found writing-material difficult to obtain, they had a way of taking old parchments which had been written many years before, and upon which the ink had faded, and writing new compositions upon them. Sometimes these palimpsests, as they are called, have been more valuable on account of the earlier writing than the later. Indeed, one of them proved to be, when examined by the microscope, a famous manuscript of Holy Scripture. Something like this has happened to Lammas Day. I do not mean that the Petrine Devotions are necessarily less important than those of the old Feast; but beneath them we discover an ancient Festival. So ancient is it that there was evidence that even in the Middle Ages its significance was forgotten. 'A curious custom at York Minster originated in the supposed association of the word "Lammas" with the word "Lambs". The tenants of the Minster brought each a live lamb to Mass on this day, as an offering to the Church to be blessed at the High Altar.'[1]

This, however, was a misreading of the word 'Lammas'. It really means 'Loaf Mass'; and is derived from a natural contraction of the Anglo-Saxon word for 'loaf'—'Hlaf' and Mass. It was the custom in very early times to make an offering of a loaf to the Church, made from wheat already gathered in, as a first-fruits thanksgiving to God. That this is the true meaning of the Feast is illustrated by the fact that in the Greek Church in earlier times the blessing of new grapes took place with elaborate ceremony; the first-fruits therefore of the vintage, as well as of the harvest, were offered to God on Lammas Day.

[1] Urlin, *Festivals, Holy Days, and Saints' Days.*

The most popular Festival in the Church of England, though it finds no place in the calendar, is the annual Harvest Festival. It is perhaps characteristic of the English people, that they prefer to thank God for the harvest when it is fully gathered in, rather than for the first-fruits. 'Come, ye thankful people, come', they sing, 'Raise the song of harvest home'.

Were the people more devout who gave God their first-fruits in hope of the future? The probability is, however, that we must go deeper even than the Catholic Church to find the origin of Lammas Day. It is most likely that it was originally a Pagan Festival, which was baptized into Christ. There are customs, especially in remote parts of the British Isles, still lingering on Lammas Day, which suggest a Pagan origin.

It was obviously the most natural thing in the world for people often living on the edge of starvation, to thank God or the gods of their faith, for the fruits of their soil. The sacrifice of Cain is an early instance of this natural instinct, and was not rejected because of the thanksgiving behind it, but for other reasons. It may well be that if Lammas Day had been in September instead of August, it would be adopted for Harvest Festivals. The real thanksgiving especially in country places today, at harvest time, often by people who only come to Church once a year, has a significance of a universal character. We do well on a special day, Lammas or otherwise, to sing

Praise, O praise our God and King!
Hymns of adoration sing.

It was my privilege on Lammas Day 1954 to worship at the beautiful church of Great Salkeld in Cumberland. By coincidence it happened that Lammas Day was also the Seventh Sunday after Trinity, when the Gospel for the day was St Mark's account of the feeding of the Four Thousand. The Rector in an admirable sermon on Lammas Day made good use of this coincidence, giving a lucid account of the narratives of the feeding of the Five Thousand and the Four Thousand; but most of all emphasizing the discourse of Jesus in Chapter 6 of St John about the Bread of Life which cometh down from Heaven to give life to the world. Though nothing is more natural than to thank God for our daily bread, we may continue to sing:

> And for richer food than this,
> Pledge of everlasting bliss:
>   Glory to the Father, Son,
>   And blessed Spirit, Three in One.

John Wesley in his sermon on the Lord's Prayer, exhorting people to thank God for their daily bread, in answer to their daily prayer, goes on to say that some of the ancient Fathers regarded the prayer for daily bread to be a prayer not only for the bread that perisheth, but for the bread that cometh down from Heaven, and consequently it was a custom, how general I do not know, for a daily celebration of Holy Communion to take place, that people might receive the spiritual food—the Bread of Heaven.

Nothing was so typical of early piety as the thanksgiving note in Holy Communion. The name 'Eucharist' simply means thanksgiving, and the prominence of thanksgiving is more conspicuous in the early liturgies than in our own. In a sense in those early days, every Eucharist was a sort of Harvest Thanksgiving. Various gifts of fruits and vegetables and other things were offered to God in thanksgiving by His people and were brought in procession by the people to the altar, where a loaf was given to the priest for consecration, and their prayer of thanksgiving, often very long, and for all sorts of gifts from God, was a conspicuous feature of the Liturgy. This thanksgiving has been greatly condensed, though very beautifully, in Western Liturgies where the officiant says, 'Let us give thanks to our Lord God', and the people respond: 'It is meet and right so to do.' And then in the Preface to the *Sanctus* the officiant says, 'It is very meet, right, and our bounden duty, that we should at all times, and in all places, give thanks unto thee, O Lord, Holy Father, Almighty, Everlasting God', and then all join with Angels and Archangels in saying 'Holy, holy, holy, Lord God of hosts...'.

Many Liturgists think that the Western Liturgies lack too much in emphasis of Offering and Thanksgiving and it is quite true that the Anglican Order of Holy Communion is essentially a Penitential Office, although it certainly culminates in triumph and joy. But with Eucharistic worship, I hope to deal in another chapter.

It is not likely that the original worship of Lammas Day will ever be restored. Other days and devotions take its place. But the joy of gratitude to God as well as its obligation must never be forgotten or ignored:

> For His mercies still endure,
> Ever faithful, ever sure.

It is a custom in a Methodist church and possibly in others to give thanks after tea meetings in a familiar verse:

> We thank thee Lord for this our food
> But more because of Jesu's blood
> Let manna to our souls be given
> The bread of Life sent down from Heaven.

This, however, is not the original form of the verse as written by Cennick. He wrote:

> We thank thee Lord for this our food
> But more for Jesu's flesh and blood
> The manna to our spirits given
> The bread of Life sent down from Heaven.

The change seems to have been made in the first half of the nineteenth century, as a result of an anti-sacramental feeling probably in reaction to the Oxford Anglo-Catholic Movement which created fear of ceremonialism in the minds of many good people.

Yet is it not appropriate that we should thank God not only for the bread that perisheth, but for the bread of Life offered to us in the Sacrament of the Lord's Supper? Ought we not always to be thankful for that richer food—

> Pledge of everlasting bliss.

CHAPTER FOUR

THE FEAST OF THE TRANSFIGURATION
(6th August)

Epistle: Peter 2¹⁶.   *Gospel:* Matthew 17¹.

'OUR PRAYING PATTERN'

'He went up into a mountain to pray and as he prayed, two men appeared and spake of his decease which he should accomplish at Jerusalem'.

LUKE 9²⁸⁻³¹.

Early in the temple met,
Let us still our Saviour greet;
NIGHTLY TO THE MOUNT REPAIR,
JOIN OUR PRAYING PATTERN THERE.
There by wrestling faith obtain
Power to work for God again.
Power His image to retrieve,
Power, like Thee, our Lord, to live.

'*Twixt the mount and multitude,*
Doing or receiving good.

'The effectual fervent prayer of a righteous man availeth much.'

JAMES 5¹⁶.

'Pray without ceasing.'

1 THESSALONIANS 5¹⁷.

THE Feast of the Transfiguration was enjoined in the year 1456 by the Church for general observance, though it had probably been celebrated in various places from the fourth century onward. It is a notable fact that this is the only incident in the active Ministry of Jesus for which such a celebration is established. Several modern writers on the Transfiguration have noticed how little attention is given to it by preachers today. To many the incident seems unintelligible, others feel that the facts are out of harmony with the scientific world in which we live. Hence we may regard the celebration of this notable Feast, if only by special annual observance, to be of real benefit to the people of God.

We have three accounts in the Gospel of the Transfiguration: two of them, those of Mark and Matthew, are identical in substance—with two or three, negligible, verbal alterations. They are purely factual accounts, without any explanation of what happened. The facts recorded are: About a week after the events at Cæsarea Philippi, Jesus took his three disciples, Peter, James, and John, into a high mountain. He was transfigured before them; his face shone and his very garments glistened. Two men, Moses and Elijah, talked with him, and Peter, not knowing what to say, uttered his much quoted words: 'Let us make three tabernacles; one for thee, and one for Moses, and one for Elijah'. A cloud overshadowed them and fear came upon them. They heard a voice saying: 'This is my beloved Son.' Then, 'suddenly, when they had looked round about, they saw no man any more, save Jesus only.'

This account, most scholars think, was given by Peter to Mark and set down by him in his Gospel. St Luke, though reciting the facts of the former records, seems to have been dissatisfied with them and to have made inquiries about this extraordinary incident in our Lord's life, and hence to have added explanations of what happened. He tells us *why* Jesus climbed the mountain. He went there to pray. He gives to us the reason of the visit of Moses and Elijah. They came to talk with Him about the decease which He should accomplish at Jerusalem, to confer with Him, that is, about His death. He adds the important information that the three disciples were heavy with sleep, which would suggest that they did not hear the conversation between Jesus and His visitors. And he particularly remarks that when they were fully awake they saw these two men leaving Him. Peter's words, blinded with excess of light as he was, are a plea that they should remain, and that the wonderful experience of divine glory should be permitted to continue. But Luke says he did not know what he was talking about. He had missed the purpose of the visit of Moses and Elijah. When overcome by fear, in the cloud, Peter heard the heavenly voice saying, 'This is my Son', would it not be a confirmation to him of his earlier intuition which he expressed at Cæsarea Philippi in answer to our Lord's question: 'Who say ye that I am?'

A modern theory, however, sees in the words of Peter at Cæsarea Philippi, 'Thou art the Christ', a memory of the voice he heard at the Transfiguration; the theory being that the Transfiguration really preceded the confession of Peter, when he answered the question of Jesus. This theory although plausible and not unattractive in itself, fails to explain the Transfiguration, and can only be supported on the assumption that the original writings have somehow become disarranged. But St Luke's narrative gives a clear account of what happened, which is really contingent on the fact that the Transfiguration succeeded the events of Cæsarea Philippi.

What is important in the modern theory is its emphasis of the parallelism between the events at Cæsarea Philippi and Mount Hermon. In each case Peter realizes that Jesus is the Messiah. In each case, he fails to see glory in the suffering Messiah; but in each case, the suffering of Jesus is emphasized. Indeed, it is that suffering which gives us a clue to the whole story of the Transfiguration. It was the prospect of that suffering which caused Jesus to go up into the mountain and pray. Our Lord's words, 'The Son of Man must suffer and die', which Peter resented as unworthy of Him, become even more significant as we realize that Moses and Elijah appeared to Him when He was praying on Mount Hermon, in order to talk with Him about that very suffering and death. The vital question to be answered is: 'Why did Jesus go up into the mountain to pray?' Peter realized the glory of the Messiah; but the thought of the suffering Messiah was so uncongenial to Him that he said, 'Be it far from thee, Lord', and received the terrible rebuke: 'Get thee behind me, Satan.' In the same way on the mount of Transfiguration, Peter missed the meaning of the divine glory, because he failed to realize that the men who appeared in glory on the mountain, came to talk to Jesus about His death. It was of course good, as the hymn says:

> . . . *to be*
> *High on the mountain here with Thee.*

but it was not good to stay there. Such experiences came not only to our Lord, but come to all men when they come, to enable them to bear the Cross.

I possess a little book, *Memoranda Sacra*, by Dr Rendel Harris, which I greatly value, not only because Dr Harris was a great scholar, but because of all the many good men I have met in my life, he stands out as the man whom one would most naturally call a saint. Of all the writings in his beautiful little devotional book, none perhaps is as valuable as his chapter on the Transfiguration. He thinks that the subject has been greatly misunderstood by commentators and too little treated by preachers, and he makes what may seem the rather amazing statement: 'There is no man who understands the Transfiguration like John Ruskin.' From a long and eloquent quotation from Ruskin, I requote the first sentences: 'We are afraid to harbour in our own hearts, or to utter in the hearing of others, any thought of our Lord as hungering, tired, or sorrowful, or having a human soul, a human will, and affected by the events of human life as a finite creature is: and yet one-half of the efficacy of His atonement and the whole of the efficacy of His example depend on His having been this to the full. Consider, therefore, the Transfiguration as it relates to the human feelings of our Lord. It was the first definite preparation for His death. . . .'

The real problem in a study of the Transfiguration is whether we begin with the divine glory, and possibly fall into the error of Peter when he said, 'Lord, it is good for us to be here', or with the human standpoint of St Luke, who says that Jesus in the moment when He realized so acutely that His lot was to suffer and die, went up into a mountain to pray. We must never forget the real humanity of Jesus. He was not God masquerading as a man. He became flesh and dwelt among us. The creeds are as emphatic in their statement that He was perfect Man—Very Man—very human—as that He was Very God of Very God. When Satan tempted Him to prove that He was the Son of God by a miracle or by the special support of Angels, He resisted the temptation. His consciousness while on earth was human consciousness. Like other men, 'He poured out groans and tears', 'He was made perfect by suffering', He was touched with the feeling of our infirmity. He was essentially a man of prayer. He lived a human life under human limitations. Differing from us in that He was a sinless man where we are sinful, He nevertheless lived a man's life. He was the only perfect man, the only true man who ever lived, because He was man as God meant man to be. But in His human life he sought divine assistance through communion with His Father—*that*, all men may seek —and refused such special supernatural help as legions of angels might give Him, in the time of His human anguish. His experience on the Mount of Transfiguration was a human experience. Acutely suffering, as He thought of the sorrow and death which was God's will for Him, He went up into the mountain to pray. And in answer to His prayer, as He was praying, Moses and Elijah came to sustain and strengthen Him.

Dr Rendel Harris writes: 'It was Christ's first preparation for death—and, therefore, to understand His Transfiguration we must understand His Crucifixion too; to see Hermon we must go to Calvary; to discern how the fashion of His countenance was altered, we must witness that other time in the garden, when "His sweat was as it were great drops of blood falling down on the ground"; to fathom how the three disciples slept through the glory, we must remember how they slept through the sorrow too. The word rendered decease is a strange one. It is literally *exodus*—"going out". They spake of this exodus which He should accomplish at Jerusalem. The same word occurs in the second epistle of Peter: "I will endeavour that ye may be able after my exodus to have these things always in remembrance"; and it is worthy of notice that the verses which follow are a reminiscence of the Transfiguration.

'We have conferences on many subjects—on peace, on holiness, on temperance; who ever heard of another conference (as this was) on *death*?'

The Greek word for decease is '*Ex Odos*'; and that is what His death meant, the deliverance and redemption of the people of God by a new exodus. Dr Rendel Harris calls the conversation of Jesus with His heavenly visitors, a 'conference on Death', and he dares to suggest the sort of things that Moses and Elijah would say to Jesus to encourage Him in that exodus which He was to accomplish at Jerusalem. Some will think that Dr Harris was too daring, and yet may it not well be that such words as his were spoken by Moses: 'I too know what it is to want not to die. I did not fear the act of dying, but the manner —away out of the Promised Land. But when I saw the will of my God in all its beauty, then even this bitter disappointment seemed bearable and the kiss of my God at the last made up for all. Death is only a kiss to those who love God; and if I had not followed the will of my God in this, what had I not lost? I had missed burial at the hands of the sons of God, and my feet would not now be standing in His presence.'

Then Elias might say: 'I had no fear of death: nay, I even prayed for it, saying, O Lord, take away my life, for I am not better than my fathers. It was not death that I feared so much as the fashion of dying when I fled from the face of Jezebel. But today I am thankful that my dying was not left to my choosing; if it had been so, I had missed the fiery chariot by which I climbed up to the presence of my King—the swift seraphic march that brought me home.'

And then Jesus might say, perhaps something like these words:

> *I wish to have no wishes left,*
> *But to leave all to thee;*
> *And yet two wills I find in Me*
> *When on My death I muse;*
> *But Lord I have a death to die,*
> *And not a death to choose.*

And so our Lord gained strength to face Calvary. His death He realized so well meant *Exodus*, the deliverance of millions of sinful men from sin, who joined together to sing:

> *Worthy the Lamb that died, they cry,*
> *To be exalted thus;*
> *Worthy the Lamb, our hearts reply,*
> *For He was slain for us.*

Peter was able to understand the glory of the shining face and dazzling raiments of his Master; but not the glory of suffering and death. Indeed, it was only slowly that men realized that the Cross of Christ was glorious; but the time was to come when the glories of the Transfiguration itself—it is perhaps not irreverent to say—would seem even less than that glory of which the author of the Epistle to the Hebrews was to speak when he said: 'We see Jesus for the suffering of death, crowned with glory and honour.'

The Transfiguration of Jesus was God's answer to His prayer. When He was praying there came to Him Moses and Elijah in glory to confer with Him about His death. He was transfigured and the brilliant light of that glory in which God's messengers came, made even His garments to be white and glistening. Those of us who have any experience of the Alpine glow, can never forget the extraordinary change when the setting sun empurples the pine trees with gorgeous colouring. This gives us some indication of what might happen in the bright light of the glory of God—'Brighter than the noon-day Sun'—even common garments dazzled the eyes of those who saw them.

Jesus did not climb Mount Hermon with the purpose of being transfigured. He climbed it to pray. Prayer is not always followed by transfiguration. In His bitter struggle in Gethsemane we look upon His 'dear disfigured face'; disfigured by sweat and blood. Yet it was here that He won the victory of Calvary; He submitted lovingly to the Will of His Father. His prayers were answered and He went forth to face His betrayal, arrest, judgement, and Crucifixion with the firm and confident step of one with a mind at peace. It was no doubt as a human being that Jesus prayed. Can we, human beings, in any way share his experience?

Charles Wesley, in one of his hymns, describes Jesus as 'our praying Pattern'. The hymn 'Holy Lamb, who Thee confess',[1] in thirty-two lines gives the profoundest and completest succinct account of what is meant by the imitation of Christ of which I have any knowledge. It summarizes the life of Jesus in the words: 'All thy life was prayer and love.' And then exhorts the followers of Christ in the following words:

> *Such our whole employment be,*
> *Works of faith and charity;*
> *Works of love on man bestowed,*
> *Secret intercourse with God.*

Do we know a truer account of the inner and outer life of Jesus and His followers than that of another couplet:

> *'Twixt the mount and multitude,*
> *Doing or receiving good*

But the fundamental fact is the fact of prayer: 'Secret intercourse with God.' This intercourse, whereby we follow the example of our 'praying Pattern', is aptly described:

> *Early in the temple met,*
> *Let us still our Saviour greet;*
> *Nightly to the mount repair,*
> *Join our praying Pattern there.*
> *There by wrestling faith obtain*
> *Power to work for God again,*
> *Power his image to retrieve,*
> *Power, like Thee, our Lord, to live.*

But is there nothing unique in the Transfiguration of our

[1] *M.H.B.*, No. 598.

Lord? Yes and No. There is nothing in it that is impossible to human experience. It is obvious that it is only as a man that Christ could pray; in this He was made like unto His brethren. But the experience is unique on account of its occasion; not because Jesus was God, but because here He prays as perfect Man with a unique mission to perform. No other man can suffer and die for the world's redemption as He was about to suffer. In these unique circumstances, God gives to Him the help of messengers particularly fitted to help Him—Moses and Elijah.

Jesus in the very hour when He so repeats and ponders on the words, 'The Son of Man must suffer and die', thought always of His followers and realized that to be His disciples, men must take up their cross and follow Him. Taking up a cross meant that the man who took it was like a criminal condemned to die, and carried upon his shoulders in the custom of those days the very instrument of his execution; and God in His mercy is the unfailing helper of those who have a cross to bear.

St Paul, at the very time that he was writing of celestial and ineffable experiences that had come to him, goes on to speak of his special prayer that he might be ridden of the thorn in his flesh. The answer that he received was: 'My grace is sufficient for thee.' On that sufficient grace in times of need, we may all depend, but depend most surely when we fall upon our knees in prayer.

Although in His humanity Our Lord has deigned to be like His brethren, our prayers must differ from His because we are sinful and He sinless. We can never pray without saying, 'God be merciful to me a sinner'; but Jesus, who offers no such prayer, says instead: 'Father forgive them, for they know not what they do.' And yet Jesus lived and died to give us privileges which He did not share. He is our praying Pattern Himself. It is quite true that when we pray, Moses and Elijah are not likely to come to our assistance; although I would be far from saying that God does not send His messengers to His lowliest followers, and the fact that I or my readers may have had no such experience is no evidence that better people have not.

The lives of the Saints, indeed, in every age record answers to
their prayers in which messengers of God have come to them.
He gives His angels charge over us to keep us in all our ways.
There may come to us no glorious vision like that of Mount
Hermon, but in prayer there are times when even we can sing:

> *The opening heavens around me shine*
> *With beams of sacred bliss,*
> *While Jesus shows His mercy mine*
> *And whispers I am His.*

Our Pattern in the Mount dwells not only on the mountain top,
but walks with us on the common road.

> *And faith has still its Olivet,*
> *And love its Galilee.*

Is there any sense in which we can share the Transfiguration
of Christ? St Paul thinks there is, since he uses the same Greek
word which is translated 'transfigured' in the Gospels in his
exhortations to the Romans and Corinthians. 'Be not conformed
to this world', he says to the Romans, 'but be ye transformed by
the renewing of your mind'[2]; and there is no lexical reason why
the Greek word translated 'transformed' should not be translated
'transfigured'. Similarly, when he speaks to the Corinthians of
their being changed 'from glory to glory, into the image of the
Lord'[2] the word 'transfigured' instead of 'changed' would
be an accurate and possibly even more appropriate translation.
Probably the word 'transformed' is the more fitting translation
since the greatest glory that can come to sinful men is to be like
Jesus, and the hope that encourages us is that one day we may
be like Him when we see Him as He is.

Transfiguration itself is in some degree a human experience.
The face of Moses shone so brightly when He conversed with
God, that the Israelites could not bear to look upon it, and as St
Paul reminds us, he was veiled. Of St Stephen, we read that when
he spoke, 'Man saw his face as if it had been the face of an angel'.

[2] Romans 12[1].   [3] 2 Corinthians 3[18].

In a very ancient book, probably of the second century, *St Paul and Thekla*, there is a description of St Paul which modern critical scholars hold to be a genuine portrait: 'A man of moderate stature, with curly hair and scanty; crooked legs; with blue eyes; and large knit eyebrows; long nose; and he was full of the grace and pity of the Lord, sometimes having the appearance of a man, but sometimes looking like an angel.' I have often wondered what St Paul looked like when as a prisoner he prayed for the Ephesian Christians. I should like to have seen his face when he spoke of the breadth and depth and height and length of the love of God and prayed that men might know the love which passeth knowledge, or when he wrote his ascription: 'Now unto him that is able to do exceeding abundantly above all that we ask or think, according to the power that worketh in us, unto him be glory . . .'[4]

I have many times in my life seen faces of very ordinary people illuminated as they prayed, particularly in simple Methodist prayer-meetings. Such shining faces of men who experience the love of God, often very simple people, must have been witnessed by some of the readers of this book.

There comes to my mind an aged woman whom I visited sixty years ago, of plain features, but deeply furrowed face, racked with rheumatism, and so poor as that the next meal was often a problem for her. I remember reading to her the 23rd Psalm; to each verse as I read it she gave vocal assent. 'I shall not want', I read, and she said, 'Thank God I have never wanted'; and so she responded verse by verse, until I came to the words: 'Surely goodness and mercy shall follow me all the days of my life.' Then that dear old creature's plain and furrowed face became positively luminous as she praised God for His unfailing mercy. I loved to talk with her about her religious experiences. The radiancy of her transfigured face as she witnessed to her joy in the Lord has left an indelible impression upon my mind.

I remember, too, a young girl, a factory hand, who sometimes prayed in public. Her face was illuminated in her prayer, and

[4] Ephesians 3[20].

her very speech transformed—the dialects and accents of her ordinary speech seemed to fall away as unconsciously when she talked with God; she chose words simple and beautiful, since she spoke the language of Israel. I was reminded of the beautiful legend of Joan of Arc, who when she went to the Dauphin's palace, surprised the courtiers that she a peasant girl should speak the French of the nobility. They accounted for it by saying that it was because of her conversation with the Saints that her speech had such an extraordinary refinement—a beautiful legend not without significance.

But it is not our Transfiguration we seek when we pray, but to do the Will of God. To seek for the joys of Transfiguration is the readiest method of losing them. The error of Peter was to desire the continuation of his enjoyment of the Divine glory, and not to realize that it came to help his Lord to bear the cross. When we go into the Mount like our Lord, it is to pray. Prayer is the mightiest lever in the world, and its lack the greatest impoverishment of religion. 'More things are wrought by prayer than this world dreams of.'

There is nothing Jesus said to His disciples with more emphasis than that they must pray, and nothing in them He criticized more strongly than their little prayer. 'The effectual fervent prayer of a righteous man availeth much.'

When we read of the scene in the Upper Room, are we not in danger of regarding as almost outside our range of thought and possibility words which our Lord expected His Disciples to take quite literally. We do well to call to mind and to ponder their significance: 'Verily, verily, I say unto you, He that believeth on me, the works that I do shall he do also; and greater works than these shall he do; because I go unto my Father. And whatsoever ye shall ask in my name, that will I do, that the Father may be glorified in the Son. If ye shall ask any thing in my name, I will do it.'[5] 'Verily, verily, I say unto you, Whatsoever ye shall ask the Father in my name, he will

[5] John 14[12-14].

give it you. Hitherto have ye asked nothing in my name: ask, and ye shall receive, that your joy may be full.'[6]

The possibilities in prayer which these words open out are almost incredible to us. 'Ye shall do greater works than I.' But this amazing promise is contingent upon continual prayer.

How then may we best keep the Feast of the Transfiguration? We do well to join with the Church of God in thanksgiving, and not to forget its secondary lesson, taught us by Peter's error. But best of all, we can keep it by a special act of prayer, some lonely vigil with God. Jesus once said to His disciples: 'Could ye not watch with me one hour?' Does He not say this to us? Great Christians have invariably found their strength in secret intercourse with God. And we shall best keep this festival of the Church by joining our praying Pattern on the mountain.

> *Pray, without ceasing pray,*
> *Your Captain gives the word;*
> *His summons cheerfully obey,*
> *And call upon the Lord:*
> *To God your every want*
> *In instant prayer display;*
> *Pray always; pray, and never faint*
> *Pray, without ceasing pray!*

[6] John 16[23-4].

CHAPTER FIVE

THE NAME OF JESUS

(7th August)

Epistle: Acts 4⁸.   *Gospel:* Luke 2²¹.

'At the Name of Jesus every knee shall bow.'

THE Festival of the Name of Jesus has two dates, the first and the most usually observed is on the Sunday between the Circumcision and the Epiphany. That it should be repeated again on 7th August is not to be wondered at, for can we rejoice too much in the precious name of Jesus.

> *To me, with Thy dear name, are given*
> *Pardon and holiness, and heaven.*

There is no more familiar quotation from Shakespeare than the words of Juliet:

> *What's in a name? that which we call a rose*
> *By any other name would smell as sweet.*

Now that names are no longer descriptive, this is of course true, but not quite true—it made a considerable difference to people in Verona whether they bore the name of Montagu or Capulet. And indeed in our own time there are 'names to conjure with'; some historical family names count for much even in England. The inheritance of a great name or a name made honourable by the deeds of one's ancestors still has meaning. I knew a young minister who bore a name honoured in his denomination, who, when he sat one day in a public place, was suddenly spoken to by the most honoured man in that denomination, who said to him: 'Somebody has just been talking to me about you. Honour your great name, honour your great name.' And then he passed on. These words had all the value of a new vocation to that young minister, who trembled at the intensity with which they were spoken and felt a quite indescribable need of new dedication to God and His work.

But it is of course true that names in modern times are not, as in ancient times, full of meaning. In the biblical stories names and natures seem to be identical, and their importance is of vital moment; for instance, the name of Jehovah—I am that I am—created a new epoch for the people of Israel. God said that Abraham, Isaac, and Jacob, who had known Him as the Lord God Almighty, did not know Him by this name which He revealed to Moses, and He commanded him to publish it with His people. It was a new name, which Israel so venerated that it was even regarded as ineffable. It was not a word to be spoken. Substitutes and synonyms were used for it. To take it in vain was a great sin. The Prophet Ezekiel even records God as saying: 'But I wrought for my name's sake, that it should not be polluted before the heathen' (Ezk 20⁹). 'It was not for your sakes, but for my holy Name's sake.' The evil deeds of the Israelites dishonoured the name Jehovah; it was for His own reputation, the honour of His name so the prophet thinks, that He helped Israel.

Nothing brings out the significance of names better than the wonderful story of the night wrestling of Jacob with his unknown foe. The main struggle seems to be a struggle of each to know the name of the other. 'Tell me thy name', says the unknown one to Jacob, and when he tells it, a new name is given to him. He is Israel because he has prevailed with God and man. But Jacob himself is as anxious to know the name of him with whom he wrestled—that name is not revealed to him. In the greatest hymn of Charles Wesley, in which the incident is so richly evangelized, and made the type of the struggle of a despairing man for salvation, the intensity of longing to know the name is expressed in the words: "Tell me Thy name and tell me now.' And gradually the penitent man, who has thought of God, as Jacob did, with fear, asks the question, 'Tell me if thy name is Love', and answers it:

'Tis Love! 'tis Love! thou diedst for me!

.   .   .   .   .

Pure, universal Love Thou art.

Now this declaration expresses both the name and the nature of God. The discovery that God is not mere fate or fear, but Love, was a discovery both of Jacob and of Charles Wesley. But we may ask whether the term 'Love' can be used as a personal designation of God. Indeed, one realizes that Wesley himself needed a personal name to express his thought, and so in the hymn he says, of Him with whom he wrestled,

I know thee, Saviour, who Thou art,
Jesus, *the feeble sinner's Friend.*

Abstract expressions like Love, though they have meaning, require more personal content if they are to be called names. Abstract qualities are sometimes, it is true, used as Christian names. I have met delightful people who were named Faith, Hope, and Charity, and other qualities too have become personal names by their use; but I have known no child named 'Love'. Often enough the word is used endearingly between lovers, or of parents to their children, but it cannot be used in a personal distinguishing way. It is rarely, if ever, used as the name of God. Expressions like 'Immortal Love, for ever full' or Tennyson's 'Strong Son of God, immortal Love' do indeed personify an abstract term, but they are rather descriptive of the nature than the *name* of God.

And so Charles Wesley, when he writes

Love divine, all loves excelling,
Joy of Heaven to earth come down,

as in the hymn already quoted, needs the name Jesus, and sings:

Jesu, Thou art all compassion,
Pure, unbounded love Thou art

It is indeed true that the name Jesus is the name above every name.

I have already gone to hymnody for my illustrations, and it is in hymnody that we best find adoration of the name of Jesus. How familiar we are with such hymns as

> *How sweet the name of Jesus sounds*
> *In a believer's ear;*

> *Jesus! the name that charms our fears,*
> *That bids our sorrows cease;*
> *'Tis music in the sinner's ears,*
> *'Tis life, and health, and peace;*

or in the great hymn of St Bernard:

> *Jesu! the very thought is sweet,*
> *In that dear name all heart-joys meet.*

But we do not exhaust the meaning of the name of Jesus when we sing of its charm and sweetness. We rightly sing:

> *All hail the power of Jesu's name;*
> *Let Angels prostrate fall;*
> *Bring forth the royal diadem*
> *And crown Him Lord of all;*

and again:

> *Jesus! the name high over all,*
> *In hell, or earth, or sky,*
> *Angels and men before it fall,*
> *And devils fear and fly.*

. . . . .

> *Jesus! the prisoner's fetters breaks,*
> *And bruises Satan's head;*
> *Power into strengthless souls it speaks,*
> *And life into the dead;*

and again:

> *Jesu's tremendous name*
> *Puts all our foes to flight:*
> *Jesus, the meek, the angry Lamb,*
> *A lion is in fight.*

It is not only a powerful name, but an authoritative one. So Peter says to the lame man: 'In the name of Jesus Christ of Nazareth, rise up and walk.'

The name was sometimes used as if it were a magic formula, and indeed if one might speak of it as 'white' and not 'black' magic, it is. Simply as a historical fact, nothing is more remarkable than the power of the name of Jesus. Truly the name of Jesus casts a spell over the minds of men. That it was regarded as magical even in early times is clear from the action of certain sorcerers in Ephesus: 'Then certain of the vagabond Jews, exorcists, took upon them to call over them which had evil spirits the name of the Lord Jesus, saying, We adjure you by Jesus whom Paul preacheth. And there were seven sons of one Sceva, a Jew, and chief of the priests, which did so.'

But let us think for a moment of the naming of Jesus. St Matthew tells us that Joseph was commanded by the Angel in his dream to call the name of the Holy Babe who was to be born 'Jesus' because He should save His people from their sins, and St Luke tells us that the Angel Gabriel told Mary to call His name 'Jesus'. A beautiful modern hymn reads:

> *And when we call Him Saviour*
> *Then we call Him by His name.*

But this of course gives the meaning of His name rather than the actual personal name which is high above every name— Jesus. The Messiah for whom the Hebrew people were looking, was to be a saviour, but a saviour from their national enemies. They did not realize that their greatest enemies were not Assyrians, Babylonians, or Romans, but their sins, though the Prophets had told them so repeatedly and emphatically.

But he was to be the Saviour, not only of the Jewish people if they would accept Him, from their sins, but to be a light to lighten the Gentiles, which, had they known it, was the greatest of all the glories of His people Israel. The name given to Jesus was prophetic in its meaning. When it was given to Him, it expressed the great hope; but there is a true sense in which He had to make His name, and He made it. No description of the way in which He made it is perhaps comparable with the words of St Paul: 'Let this mind be in you, which was also in Christ Jesus: who being in the form of God, thought it not robbery to be equal with God: but made himself of no reputation, and took upon him the form of a servant and was made in the likeness of men: and being found in fashion as a man, he humbled himself, and became obedient unto death, even the death of the cross. Wherefore God also hath highly exalted him, and given him a name which is above every name: that at the name of Jesus every knee should bow, of things in heaven, and things in earth, and things under the earth; and that every tongue should confess that Jesus Christ is Lord, to the glory of God the Father' (Philippians 2[5-11]).

Do we realize that the name 'Jesus' was a common, and even a commonplace name when it was given to Him, a name that many Jewish children were given? The Jewish form of it is Joshua, and although there was an Israelite chieftain of that name, the name was in ordinary use. Our Lord, however, made it unique. When we name children today, we do not call them Jesus. It is a universal intuition to leave that name, high over all, to the Saviour of the world.

That a special day should be observed to adore the name of Jesus is natural and right, and yet to Christians their adoration can be confined to no one day. And it is true, of course, that the highest adoration we can give Him is by imitation of Him, and humble gratitude to Him in our normal lives. But in our worship, the forms of adoration should not be ignored; for instance, it is the custom of the great majority of Christians to bow their heads and bend their knees at the mention of the name of Jesus in the Creed: 'At the Name of Jesus every knee shall bow.'

The Methodist people, who are naturally the most likely to read this book, do not very usually observe this ritual. Indeed they appear to be afraid of it, so much so that in their hymn-books, they have even altered the words of this familiar hymn I have just quoted, from '*At* the Name . . .' to '*In* the Name of Jesus every knee shall bow', thus misquoting the Scripture. It may not be known to them all that John Wesley, in his early days, always bowed at the name of Jesus in the Creed, and there is good evidence, though it is true that it is but on a scrap of paper,[1] that he preserved this custom after his Evangelical conversion. Of course it is quite possible that some people who observe a ritual fail to observe what is much more important, adoration in life of Jesus; but the fear of rite and the consequent lack of gestures of reverence have gone too far amongst us. To bow at the name of Jesus is surely a beautiful acknowledgement of His claim to the adoration of His people. Any way in which it is possible to express our love and thanksgiving for the name He has made so glorious should be used by all who sing: 'O come, let us adore Him, Christ the Lord.'

There is nothing so precious as the name of Jesus, and what it means, and will mean for ever to Mankind; and for my part I would re-echo the words of Charles Wesley:

> *Happy, if with my latest breath*
> *I may but gasp His name;*
> *Preach Him to all, and cry in death:*
> *Behold, behold the Lamb!*

[1] J. E. Rattenbury, *Conversion of the Wesleys*, p. 223.

CHAPTER SIX

ST BARTHOLOMEW'S DAY

(24th August)

Epistle: Acts 5¹². *Gospel suggested:* John 1⁴³⁻⁵¹.

'Come and see.'
'Search and look.'

TO most minds the day of St Bartholomew is associated with horror and massacre. That the name of St Bartholomew should have such an association is very contrary to the character of the quiet, studious, and reflective Saint Nathanael. There can be little doubt that Nathanael is the same man as Bartholomew. The name Bartholomew is what today we should call a surname —it simply means son of Tolmai. The word Bar is a suffix, just as the word 'son'—Thomson, Johnson—is in our language an affix. The suffixes 'Mac', 'O', and 'Ap', are the Scotch, Irish, and Welsh equivalents of 'Bar'. We should not have known that Peter's surname was Barjona except for one well-known saying of Jesus. It is evident that the identification of Bartholomew and Nathanael was unknown to the selectors of the Gospels and Epistles for St Bartholomew's Day, for those which have been chosen would be suitable for any apostle. There can be no doubt that the true Gospel for the day is John 2⁴³⁻⁵¹, the narrative of the call of Nathanael.

Nathanael seems to have been sitting under the shadow of a fig tree on some summer day, reflectively reading and musing over what he read. His enthusiastic friend Philip disturbed his meditation with his words: 'We have found him, of whom Moses in the law, and the prophets, did write, Jesus of Nazareth, the son of Joseph.' To which proclamation Nathanael sceptically replied: 'Can there any good thing come out of Nazareth?' Philip would not stop to argue; he was a practical man, who had too often argued unsuccessfully with his quiet friend Nathanael. He was too impatient to try again, but almost roughly said:

'Come and see.' Nathanael, overwhelmed by the evident conviction of Philip, rose up and followed him and so saw Jesus, and when he found Him, his first discovery was that Jesus had already seen him and read his heart and thoughts.

What was Nathanael reading or thinking about under the fig tree? There can be little doubt, I think, that it was the story of Jacob, to which story several allusions were made by Jesus. Nathanael did not like that crafty man Jacob, and had no wish to be like him, and yet when he thought of the wrestler at Peniel who in his struggle with that Unknown was named Israel, a man who had prevailed both with men and with God, Nathanael longed to be such a man. Jesus understood his aspiration, and exclaimed: 'Behold an Israelite indeed, in whom is no guile'—that is to say, an Israel in whom there is no Jacob. When Nathanael realized that our Lord had read the inmost thoughts of his heart, he cried out: 'Rabbi, thou art the son of God; thou art the King of Israel.' And then came from Jesus the further evidence that it was of Jacob that Nathanael had been reading or thinking, and of Jacob's ladder, for He said: 'Verily, verily, I say unto you, Hereafter ye shall see heaven open, and the angels of God ascending and descending upon the Son of man.'

A forgotten hymn of Charles Wesley gives beautiful expression to the meaning of this verse:

> *What doth the ladder mean,*
> *Sent down from the Most High?*
> *Fasten'd to earth its foot is seen,*
> *Its summit to the sky:*
> *Lo! up and down the scale*
> *The angels swiftly move,*
> *And God, the great Invisible,*
> *Himself appears above!*
>
> *Jesus that ladder is,*
> *The incarnate Deity,*
> *Partaker of celestial bliss*
> *And human misery;*

Sent from His high abode,
To sleeping mortals given,
He stands, and man unites to God,
And earth connects with heaven.

Philip the practical man seems to have been rather rough and violent when he heard the satirical question of the theorist, Nathanael: 'Can there any good thing come out of Nazareth?' Philip was moved by realized fact and experience, and impatient with the quibbles of a theorist. He cared for fact. His later words, 'Show us the Father, and it sufficeth us' (John 14⁸), are a characteristic demand of the man who wanted explicit and factual statements. He was quite a good arithmetician. He knew perfectly well that if you distributed five loaves among five thousand people, there would only be a crumb for each. But the higher arithmetic of love, by which division is turned into multiplication, was a branch of mathematics unknown to this practical person. In this interview with Nathanael, however, we see the practical man on his good side, the man who prizes fact rather than theory. 'Come and see,' he says; see for yourself, make the experiment and you will not fail in the experience.

In these days in which I am writing, great excitement has been caused by a learned lady who would teach children morality without religion. While the controversy may well be forgotten before this book is published, it is interesting to inquire why many scientists are unscientific in their approach to Christianity. Science has won its magnificent triumphs by experiment, and scientists accept no theory without testing it by experiment; but how many of those who reject Christ have made the one experiment necessary? Why do they not come and see? Too often they assume that the Christian hypothesis is impossible, and some prejudice like that of Nathanael, the result it may be of research, prevents them from making the experiment which to many millions of people has brought conviction and experience.

Take for instance a question like the Resurrection of Jesus.

Having come to the conclusion beforehand that it is impossible for men to rise from the dead, they do not even examine the Christian evidences for the Resurrection. On account of their foregone conclusion, they reject the Christian conception that a unique person may be an exception to a general rule; that is to say, they beg the question. If they do consider these evidences, it is only to explain them away. And yet even secular historians agree that the Church of God came into existence because the disciples believed that Jesus had risen from the dead. Can a fact of this sort be really due to a delusion of so many people? One great scientist of the nineteenth century taught that the fundamental need was to sit down before fact as a little child. The words of Philip to Nathanael are forceful still. To refuse to come and see is to refuse, in the most important of all spheres, the scientific method of experiment. I know well the answer that some might make. 'Where shall we come and see?' We have come to the Church and we have seen what fails to impress us. We have met men and women who do not seem to us to be better in character than many unbelievers. And this Christians know too well is true. Do we not all feel sometimes that we are mere caricatures of our Saviour? Do we not all need continually to pray: 'God be merciful to us sinners'? But still, those who have merely seen the caricatures of Christ have not come and seen Him.

The mere 'Fact of Christ', as the admirable book of Dr Carnegie Simpson with that title suggests, is in itself something inexplicable. A friend of mine told me the other day of an interesting talk he had some thirty years ago, with a well-known agnostic who after expressing his disbelief in Christianity, said: 'There are three things which to me cannot be explained: Jesus of Nazareth, Francis of Assisi and Joan of Arc. Has any scientist really explained them?' Mrs Humphrey Ward, in her autobiography, records a conversation she had with Walter Pater, whom she had known at Oxford in earlier days and who was supposed to have been a rationalist. To her surprise he said: 'I cannot agree with some of your views, there is something mysterious about Jesus which you cannot explain—there is mystery—how could an ordinary man have said: 'Come unto me, all ye that labour and are heavy laden, and I will give you rest'? The best answer is: 'Come and see.'

Who are the people who say 'Come and see'? Like Philip, they are the people who themselves have come and seen. 'But Peter and John answered and said unto them, Whether it be right in the sight of God to hearken unto you more than unto God, judge ye. For we cannot but speak the things which we have seen and heard.'

These men were not merely giving their witness to the Jesus of history, but also to the Christ of experience, whose living presence they had realized on the day of Pentecost—an experience that equipped them to preach the Gospel from Jerusalem to the ends of the earth. And so men in our own days who have come and seen repeat Philip's words. Of such words there is no better example in modern times than the magnificent defence of his faith that Charles Wesley gave in a great hymn:

> *What we have felt and seen*
> *With confidence we tell,*
> *And publish to the sons of men*
> *The signs infallible.*

Can Christian experience be put more succinctly and triumphantly than by another couplet in this hymn?

> *But us you never can persuade*
> *That honey is not sweet.*

Truly we are compassed about with a great cloud of witness, men of all generations who have tasted and seen how gracious the Lord is, and with one voice they say: 'Come and see.'

An interesting parallel with the story of Nathanael is the incident in Chapter 7 of St John, of the attempted arrest of Jesus by the Pharisees' police, and the intervention of Nicodemus. The officers who had been sent to arrest Jesus returned without him.

'Never man spake as this man', they said. The personality of Jesus mastered them. The Pharisees, angry and disgusted at the failure of their police, scornfully asked them if any of the rulers of the Pharisees had accepted Jesus. It was at this point that Nicodemus, himself a Pharisee, intervened: 'Doth our law judge any man, before it hear him, and know what he doeth?' The Pharisees replied: 'Art thou also of Galilee? Search, and look: for out of Galilee ariseth no prophet.'

It is quite plain that the Pharisees held the same opinion as Nathanael, a man who had searched much, held: that nothing could be found in Scripture to justify the claim of the Galilean to be the Messiah. Indeed it was a foregone conclusion that no good could come out of Nazareth. It is also noticeable that the police officers, like Nathanael, were overcome by the personality of Jesus when they saw his face and heard him speak.

Nicodemus was silent when the Pharisees reproached him and told him to search and look. He could have answered them, for he had spent much time, searching and looking; but in recent days, since the memorable night when he stole to Jesus, he not only searched but found. He could not forget that dark night, when the chamber in which he met Jesus was illuminated by the 'Light of the World'. How often would he call to memory the reproaches of Jesus, but even more, the comfortable words: 'And as Moses lifted up the serpent in the wilderness, even so must the Son of man be lifted up: that whosoever believeth in him should not perish, but have eternal life'!

Did he not also hear the words that many people think the most precious words of Jesus: 'For God so loved the world, that he gave his only begotten Son, that whosoever believeth in him should not perish, but have everlasting life'?

When Nicodemus came by night and saw Jesus, he discovered, through that experience, a clue unknown to the Pharisees, by which he could interpret the Scriptures.

'Search and look', says the theorist, and 'Come and see', says the practical man. Are these two sayings mutually exclusive?

On the contrary, the early Christians found in Jesus their clue. If a man has no clue when in a labyrinth or maze, he is likely to lose his way. The old Testament, the only Scriptures which were available in Apostolic times, are a sort of labyrinth. No one need be surprised that it was necessary to ask an intelligent man, like the Ethiopean eunuch: 'Understandest thou what thou readest?' The Old Testament is not a book, but a library which took a thousand years to write. It is an extraordinary amalgam of history and folk lore, prose and poetry, drama and lyric, the greatest hymns in the world (the Book of Psalms), common sense, proverbial philosophy, and that form of literature peculiar to Hebrew writers which we call prophecy. Merely regarded as literature, it reaches higher levels in certain passages than any ancient literature, but above all it is a book of religion, recording revelations of God, which though partial, are of unique and abiding value. The Pharisees described their scriptures summarily as 'the Law and the Prophets'. One of the noblest of them, a century or so before, wrote that he meditated in the Law, day and night. But in the time of our Lord, this meditation fixed itself, amongst the Scribes, on external details of ritual and conduct. They had much more to say of the tithing of 'mint, anise, and cummin', than of the weightier things of the Law. They realized, no doubt, that the Scripture was the history of their own race and contained the highest expression both of its literary genius and its prophetic insight. It must be admitted that they saw and preached the guidance of God in the history of Israel. They pondered alike on His great mercies, His severe punishment when they forsook Him, and the lovingkindness with which He received them when they returned to Him once again; and they rightly sang:

> *Oh that men would praise the Lord for his goodness,*
> *And for his wonderful works to the children of men!*

They realized that they were the chosen people of God under his special direction and care. Notwithstanding the terrible disasters and exile to which they had been subjected, they retained their faith in God and believed that they, as His people, would not only be saved from the power of their mighty enemies, but were destined to prevail over other nations; and they looked to the future coming of the Messiah as a climactic day in their history. They found in the prophets encouragement for their hope of final conquest, whatever temporary defeat they had to endure. They saw much and have put the whole world under a perpetual debt to them by their preservation of Holy Scriptures, but they did not possess the true clue to interpretation.

Modern scholars, through their examination of the text of the Old Testament, have done much to illuminate the historical and literary problems which confront the students of our day. The disclosure of the underlying sources which were combined by Jewish editors to make the historical books has been generally accepted. The discovery of writings of different periods in some of the prophetical books, especially that of Isaiah which hitherto had been attributed to a single writer, has solved many historical and literary problems. These scholars have been successful in dating the various books of the Scriptures and arranging the texts in such a way as to make the Old Testament a much more attractive book. But these important historical and literary discoveries are only of secondary value. The Old Testament is primarily by far the greatest religious book that has come to us from pre-Christian centuries. The Holy Scriptures are not a mere collection of ancient Jewish writings, but are revelations of the Living God. These Scriptures contain the Word of the Lord. Spiritual things must be spiritually discerned; and so it comes to pass that simple souls—babes and sucklings— discover in the Bible the saving truths which are often hidden from the wise and prudent. The Christian clue, when used even by the wayfaring man, though a fool, is the most important key to the deep spiritual problems with which the Old Testament deals.

It is therefore not surprising that our Lord Himself said to the scribes and Pharisees of His day: 'Search the scriptures; for in them ye think ye have eternal life: and they are they which testify of me: And ye will not come to me, that ye might have life,' (John 5³⁹). We can see how the words of Philip to Nathanael, 'Come and see', provide a clue for those who search and look. But 'when He came to his own, His own received him not'.

The early Christians found the clue in Jesus. As the New Testament shows us, they found Jesus everywhere in the Old Testament. They saw that whereas the Pharisees emphasized merely the externalities of the Law, Jesus seized its essential inner truths, restating the Law and yet not destroying but fulfilling it: 'For the law was given by Moses, but grace and truth came by Jesus Christ.'

Over and over again, especially in the Gospels of Matthew and John, we find the claim that Old Testament sayings were fulfilled in the life of Jesus. Nothing could be more revolutionary than the interpretation given by the first Christians, of the Old Testament. How grotesque it must have seemed to the learned Jews of that day to be told that this Galilean artisan was the real clue to interpretation of the Scriptures on which their Rabbis had spent so many long and patient hours of research!

The Christian method of interpretation is clearly shown in the incident of Philip and the Ethiopian eunuch, whom he saw sitting in his chariot, reading the Scripture. Philip asked him: 'Understandeth thou what thou readest?' The passage he was reading was in Isaiah: 'He was led as a sheep to the slaughter; and like a lamb dumb before his shearers, so opened he not his mouth. . . .' 'And the eunuch answered Philip, and said, I pray thee, of whom speaketh the prophet this? of himself, or of some other man? Then Philip opened his mouth, and began at the same scripture, and preached unto him Jesus.'

The New Testament abounds in such interpretations of Scripture. Thus the early Christians did not fail to search and look, but it was because they came and saw that they understood the Scriptures.

The Scribes of our Lord's time, did not think that Chapter 53 of Isaiah, which the Ethiopian was reading, was even a

Messianic prophesy; but did not Jesus, and Jesus only, fulfill the words, 'He was wounded for our transgressions, he was bruised for our iniquities: and with his stripes we are healed'? Christians sought for Jesus in the Old Testament and they found Him. The prophesies which they saw fulfilled in Him were not fulfilled in the way in which they expected them to be. They expected a royal Prince of terrible power, coming from heaven to destroy the enemies of Israel, the people of God; but He came, the babe of a lowly maid, heralded by Angels, who said: 'Peace On earth peace, good will toward Men.' Judgement was what the Jews expected of the Messiah, as they read their ancient Scriptures; but Jesus came, not 'to condemn the world; but that the world through him might be saved.' They expected the exaltation of their own nation; but it was the *world* that God so loved. Jesus was the real glory of His people Israel, because He was the light to lighten the Gentiles.

One of the early Christian writers, wrote: 'God, who at sundry times and in divers manners [or, as it has been translated, 'in bits and fragments'] spake in time past unto the fathers by the prophets, hath in these last days spoken unto us by his Son.'

The bits and fragments of the Old Testament Revelations are integrated in Jesus. It is as if the Old Testament, by its partial revelations was spelling the word 'JESUS'. Here we see a 'J', there an 'E', somewhere else an 'S', in another place a 'U'; but the letters of the name are disjointed. They only came together in the name JESUS when the WORD was made flesh and dwelt among us. Everything in the Old Testament revelation paves the way to Jesus. He is the final Revelation of God. Where Moses could only get a glimpse of His glory, the Disciples 'beheld his glory . . . full of grace and truth'.

The disciples of Jesus were slow of heart to believe, and only gradually saw Him. Even after His Resurrection, they were the victims of their foregone conclusions that He would restore power to Israel, and asked when that restoration should take place. It was because they showed that they were still mundane in spirit, that Jesus refused to permit them to witness to Him

before the Holy Ghost came upon them; and it was not till the
day of Pentecost that the scales entirely dropped from their
eyes. Then they realized that Jesus of Nazareth was not only
their historical friend in Galilee, but Alpha and Omega, the
beginning and the end: and they knew when they went to the
ends of the world to preach His Gospel, He Himself would be
with them.

This Jesus, the same yesterday, today, and for ever, has always
been the clue of Christians to an interpretation of the Old
Testament. It was used alike by the Fathers of the Church, the
Medieval devotional writers, and the great English Protestant
hymnists of the eighteenth century. Sometimes Bernard of
Clairvaux has been criticized for finding Jesus in an erotic
Oriental love song, the Song of Solomon; but Jesus is to be
found in and through human love. The great hymn-writers of
the eighteenth century always found Jesus in the Old Testament.
For instance, Dr Watts, in his noble paraphrase of Psalm 72,
which describes an ideal king, boldly but naturally writes in the
familiar words,

> *Jesus shall reign where'er the sun*
> *Doth his successive journeys run,*

and applies to Jesus the oriental symbols of royalty which the
Psalm contains. Charles Wesley deals similarly with Psalm 45,
which describes the glory of the Israelitish king and his foreign
bride. He finds in this noble psalm, Jesus and His Church; and
the reason, as he sings, is that his 'heart is full of Christ, and longs
its glorious matter to declare'.

So throughout Christian history, Jesus is found in the Old
Testament. The kingdom of Israel is regarded as coming to
its glory in the birth of the Child of Bethlehem. The men who
saw Jesus were the men who found Him, throughout the history
of His native country, *yesterday* the same as today and for ever.

CHAPTER SEVEN

HOLY CROSS

(14th September)

Epistle: Philippians 2⁵.   *Gospel:* John 12³¹.

'And I, if I be lifted up from the earth, will draw all men unto me.'
JOHN 12³².

TWO Festival Days in the calendar are set apart for the veneration of the Holy Cross. The earlier, 3rd May, is called the 'Invention (the finding) of the Holy Cross'; the later, the feast of 14th September, is named 'The Exaltation of the Cross'.

There seems no valid reason for denying that the Empress Helena visited Jerusalem in the hope of finding the Cross. But the story of the discovery is a legend about whose truth there is necessarily a difference of opinion. I will quote here a succinct account of the origin of the 'Invention' of the Cross:

'The Holy Sepulchre had been filled up with rubbish, and the Emperor Hadrian had built a temple to Venus on the site. Constantine wished to build a church there, and his mother Helena, though almost eighty years of age, determined herself to visit the Holy Land, and seek the Cross, concerning which she had had a vision. After diligent search and many difficulties, the aged Empress was rewarded with the [alleged] discovery of three buried crosses, and that which had borne the Saviour, was identified by a miracle—namely, the healing of a sick person who touched it. Some of the True Cross Helena left at Jerusalem, where it was kept in a silver case and venerated every year by the faithful; some, on her way home, she gave to the city of Constantinople, and brought the rest to Rome, where the Church of "Santa Croce in Gerusalemme" was built to enshrine it.'[1]

[1] *Festivals, Holy Days, and Saints' Days*, Ethel Urlin.

The evidence that the Cross found was the True Cross, while it would fail to convince the modern critic, seems to have convinced the Empress. That ceremonies of veneration of the Holy Cross commenced in Rome in A.D. 327 in the reign of Constantine is some confirmation of the historicity of the activities of the Empress Helena.

The ceremonies at Jerusalem were more elaborate than those at Rome and had a local significance; for processions along the Via Dolorosa to Calvary made realization of the tragedy of the Cross more vivid. All over Europe, repetitions of these ceremonies, not unnaturally, sprang to birth.

The exaltation of the Cross was due to later events. In A.D. 614 Jerusalem was taken by the Persians, and for thirteen years the Relic remained in Persia with the captive Emperor Heraclius. There was such universal joy at its return (A.D. 627) that a festival called 'The Exaltation of the Cross' was established in commemoration and kept annually as the anniversay of its restoration

The religious value of these observances, recalling as they did the crucifixion of our Lord, cannot be denied, for as the Gospel of the day reminds us, Jesus Himself said: 'I, if I be lifted up from the earth, will draw all men unto me.' Reverence and true veneration were undoubtedly created in devout minds by the exaltation of the Cross. Unfortunately, however, the fact which was most prized by almost all the people who took part in them was the discovery of a miracle-working relic. As the *Catholic Encyclopedia* reminds us, the abuse of relics went very far. The veneration of a relic of such value as the True Cross issued probably in more abuse than any other such ceremony.

Manufacture of pieces of the True Cross was a profitable industry in the Middle Ages. As I have shown in Chapter 1, there was an ancient conception of an efflux issuing from the body of a Saint to anything with which he had been in touch; and the Cross on which the Saviour Himself was crucified could hardly fail to be estimated as having more miraculous virtue than other relics. This superstition, as we think it, perhaps suggests a question as to the wisdom of the Anglican Reformers in retaining the Festival of the Holy Cross. Yet however much of superstition may have characterized the celebrations of earlier days, there must always have been many people who when they venerated the Cross adored the Crucified.

Nothing can be more revered by Christian people than the Cross of our Redemption. But the truth that I want to emphasize is that St Paul and not St Helena was the real discoverer of the Cross. He was the first man to glory in the Cross, the memory of which was so great a tragedy to early Christians. St Paul realized that the very infamy of the Cross was its glory, and his challenge to the world, 'God forbid that I should glory, save in the cross of our Lord Jesus Christ', was an innovation of a surprising character to his contemporaries.

There are good reasons for believing that the Epistle to the Galatians was written as early as A.D. 49,[2] though the generally accepted opinion is that it was written four or five years later than this; but there can be little doubt that St Paul was the first man to realize the glory of the Cross. In the early sermons of St Peter in the Acts of the Apostles, the Crucifixion is referred to very little. It has often been noticed that Peter never uses the word Cross; the memory of Calvary was too poignant. His stress and indeed the stress of the early Missionary speeches even of St Paul, is rather on the Resurrection than the Cross. The reference of St Stephen to the Cross was made in order to censure the Jews for crucifying Jesus as their Fathers had persecuted the Prophets.

Much the earliest historical reference to the Cross as glorious is that of St Paul. In the defiant challenge he made to his contemporaries in his words: 'God forbid that I should glory, save in the Cross of our Lord Jesus Christ, by whom the world is crucified unto me, and I unto the world', we find a new Calvary. Here in St Paul's experience stand three crosses: the central Cross in which he glories, that of St Paul himself ('the chief of sinners') corresponding to the cross of the penitent thief, and that of the world, which like the impenitent thief, died, I am sure,

[2] See W. H. Lake, *Early Epistles of St Paul*.

'railing'. St Paul in these words is not glorying so much in the death of Christ as in the infamous instrument on which he died. When Dr Isaac Watts, in his great hymn, paraphrases St Paul's words,

> Forbid it, Lord, that I should boast,
> Save in the death of Christ, my God,

he hardly catches the significance of Paul's use of the word Cross.

The significance of the apostle's discovery of the Cross becomes plainer when we recall his other great words to the Galatians: 'I am crucified with Christ: nevertheless I live; yet not I, but Christ liveth in me: and the life which I now live in the flesh I live by the faith of the Son of God, who loved me, and gave himself for me.

Nor must we forget his determination, of which he reminded the Corinthians, 'not to know any thing among you, save Jesus Christ, and him crucified'. His Gospel of the Cross, as he says, was to the Greeks foolishness and to the Jews a scandal, a stumbling-block. Paul gloried that he bore branded on his body the marks of Christ crucified.

(1)   It is really difficult today, because of the reverence we all give to the Cross of Christ, to realize sharply the infamy of crucifixion, and the horror with which men regarded it. If we are to think of it as the men who witnessed it and suffered it thought of it, a real effort of historical imagination is needed to reproduce in our minds the horror and foulness of crucifixion. The only parallel that I can think of, and that lacks the cruelty of crucifixion, is the gallows. I have sometimes thought that the quite horrible picture by Hogarth of the mob at an execution at Tyburn gives to us a better conception of what the Cross really was, than the pictures of Calvary by the great artists who present to us beautiful expressions of piety and love. It is true that they often give us pictures of the agony of the crucified Saviour, but does one of them excite the horror which Hogarth's

Tyburn picture excites? More often, they express the devotion of the lovers of the Saviour. Such works as those of Fra Angelico and Il Perugino appeal to the deepest sense of Christian gratitude and love; but the infamy of Calvary is swallowed up in the victory of the exalted Saviour whose Cross we know to be the throne from which, as even Napoleon Bonaparte said, He rules more men than any other Emperor of history. To the Jews the Cross was a cursed thing; it was the form of execution that was given to the foulest of people. There was nothing honourable about crucifixion; the feeling men had of it was similar to our feeling about the gallows. Though execution was always terrible, there were honourable as well as dishonourable executions in English history. Decapitation was considered honourable —the lot of rebellious princes and aristocrats—but the gallows, with the ribald mob around, was, alas, often a centre of disgusting entertainment for a brutal British crowd, for such a crowd, indeed, as Hogarth depicts. An instance of the hatred of this infamous form of death can be found in the Nuremberg trials. Goering, for example, could have tolerated being shot like a soldier, but the thought of the gallows infuriated him. The Crucifixion was just as infamous, with the added horror of its almost diabolical cruelty. This was the feeling which no doubt St Paul shared with his contemporaries—Christian, Jewish, and Pagan. When he said that he gloried in anything so infamous as the Cross, his words must have startled, and probably shocked, those who first heard them. And yet how right he was! He discovered, in the depths of degradation to which Jesus descended on the Cross, the unscalable heights of Divine Compassion and Love. The great passage selected as the Epistle for Holy Cross Day describes stage by stage the descent of one who counted it not a prize to be on an equality with God, but emptied himself of all but Love, and became a man, a servant, and even a crucified slave, because He loved men so deeply. His very descent to the depths of degradation are realized by Paul to be the supreme proof of His love, and it was in that unutterable love that Paul was glorying. He tells us much about the precious death of Christ, but here it is the actual instrument of His death, the Cross, in which he glories, that he finds his deepest love. His vision of the Cross as glorious was so true that everybody today realizes it and finds it difficult to think vividly of the historical degradation of Calvary.

(2) *The Cross of St Paul*

I believe St Paul, 'the chief of sinners' as he calls himself, thought of his own cross as corresponding to that of the Penitent thief. He knew the words of Jesus, 'If any man will come after me, let him . . . take up his cross, and follow me', and like a condemned criminal, he had taken up his cross and followed Jesus until he came to the Calvary where he was crucified. He actually rejoices that in some sense he can suffer as his Saviour did; so he says: 'Now I rejoice in my sufferings for your sake, and fill up on my part that which is lacking of the afflictions of Christ in my flesh for his body's sake, which is the church.'[3]

In his great apologia, in the second epistle to the Corinthians, he discusses the things in which he can glory. He recites facts in which he might glory but will not. What he does glory in is his infirmities. In the defence he makes of his own Apostolate against those who deny it, he recites in a memorable passage the many sufferings he has endured, stripes, imprisonments, shipwrecks, trouble with the Churches and many other things. Such a recital of sufferings might at first sight almost suggest pride in his heroism; but actually he recites them because they were to him crucifixion with Christ, and in that he always glories. As he says, he glories not in his rich endowment of mind, but in his infirmities: when he is weak, then he is strong. Once, it is true, suffering from a thorn in the flesh, he prays for relief, which apparently he does not receive, but he does receive the grace 'which is sufficient' for him. It seems almost incredible at first sight to think that his sufferings and infirmities should make him rejoice, and yet his glory in being crucified with Christ is plainly sincere.

[3] Colossians 1[24].

Is it not a notable fact that he seems never happier than when in prison? It is then that he says to the Philippians, 'Rejoice, again I say rejoice', and says it because he was so happy himself. The heights of rapture to which he rises are never sublimer than in his prison days. He rises as it were above himself when he writes to the Ephesians from prison. There is the grim story, written by Poe, of a man, suffering under the Inquisition, who was placed in a contracting chamber; in terror he saw the walls moving around him, gradually contracting to crush him slowly to death. Paul's prison seems rather an expanding chamber into which the glory of God descends, until he sees his great vision of the Father of every family in heaven and earth, and of the love of Christ in its height and depth and breadth and length, which passeth knowledge. Here is rejoicing in tribulation, and glorying in the Cross. He finds joy and glory in his degradation and infirmity. Always he might be saying: 'God forbid that I should glory, save in the cross of our Lord Jesus Christ.'

In one of the most beautiful books in the world, the *Fioretti* (Little Flowers) of St Francis of Assisi, we have in the eighth, and I think most beautiful chapter, an account of similar teaching by St Francis. It is a story which Brother Leo, who unlike most of his brethren lived to be a very old man, must have loved to tell when talking to his brethren about his great Saint and hero. Space, unfortunately, makes it necessary for me to condense it. Francis and Leo were walking one icy cold day from Perugia to the Church of St Mary of the Angels near Assisi, where there seems to have been some hostel or convent. It was a long walk, about eight miles, in bitterly cold weather. Anyone who has felt the bitterness of the Tremontana wind in that district can well imagine the sufferings of these two men on a bitter winter day. As they walked (and here I condense), Francis, after a silence, said, 'Brother Leo, if the Brothers Minor were good examples of holiness and edification to all men, this would not be the perfect joy', and then walked on. And after a little time he addressed Leo again, and said: 'If the Brothers Minor

could heal all diseases, give the dumb to speak and the blind to
see, this would not be the perfect joy.' And he walked on. But
after a time he said again: 'Brother Leo, if the Brothers Minor
had all the knowledge of Scripture and philosophy and knew
the secrets of men's souls, write that in all this would not be the
perfect joy.' After another pause he cried: 'Brother Leo, thou
little sheep of God, if the Brothers Minor had a perfect
knowledge of all animals, birds and of the flowers and fruits of
the earth [as we should say, of botany and physiology], this
would not be the perfect joy.' And again after an interval he
said: 'If the Brothers Minor had so great eloquence that they
could convert the infidel, even this would not be the perfect joy.'
So they walked on through piercing wind and falling snow until
at last, Brother Leo said: 'Father, prithee in God's name, tell
me wherein is perfect joy to be found?' And St Francis answered
him thus: 'If when we are come to St Mary of the Angels, wet
through with rain, frozen with cold, foul with mire and tor-
mented with hunger; and when we knock at the door, the
doorkeeper cometh in a rage and says "Who are ye?", and we
say: "We are two of your brothers", and he answeres: "Ye are
no true men; ye are rather two knaves that go deceiving the
world and stealing the alms of the poor; begone"; and he
openeth not to us, and maketh us stay outside hungry and cold
all night in the rain and snow; then if we endure patiently such
cruelty, such abuse, and such insolent dismissal without com-
plaint or murmuring, and believe humbly and charitably that
that doorkeeper truly knows us, and that God maketh him to
rail against us; O Brother Leo, write that there is perfect joy.
And,' added Francis, 'if, after repeated knockings and constant
dismissals by the porter, constrained by hunger and by cold,
we knock once more and pray with many tears that he open
to us for the love of God and let us but come inside, and he
more insolently than ever crieth, "These be impudent rogues,
I will pay them out as they deserve"; and issues forth with a big
knotted stick and seizes us by our cowls and flings us on the
ground and rolls us in the snow, bruising every bone in our

bodies with that heavy stick; if we, thinking on the agony of the blessed Christ, endure all these things patiently and joyously for love of Him; write, O Brother Leo, that here and in this, perfect joy is found. And now Brother Leo hear the conclusion. Above all the grace and the gifts of the Holy Spirit that Christ giveth to His beloved is that of overcoming self, and for love of Him willingly to bear pain and buffetings and revilings and discomfort; for in none other of God's gifts save these, may we glory, seeing they are not ours, but of God. Wherefore the Apostle saith, "What hast thou that is not of God, and if thou hast received it of Him, wherefore dost thou glory, as if thou hadst it of thyself?" But in the cross of tribulation and of affliction we may glory, because this is ours. Therefore the Apostle saith: "I will not glory, save in the cross of our Lord Jesus Christ." '

St Francis echoes precisely what St Paul claims he gloried in his infirmities; but does this seem possible to us today. Neither Paul nor Francis were miserable men. Nothing characterizes St Francis more than his joyousness. He did not wish people to be miserable. He called his Brothers Minor, '*Joculatories dei*' (Minstrels of God). No one rejoiced in lovely things more than he as his famous hymn shows, in which God is praised for sun, and moon, and water, and natural things.

What is the secret of this glorying and joy in the Cross of Christ? St Paul solves this problem in his other great saying: 'I am crucified with Christ: nevertheless I live; yet not I, but Christ liveth in me: and the life which I now live in the flesh I live by the faith of the Son of God, who loved me, and gave himself for me.'

St Paul was so united with the Saviour who had risen again from the dead and was a living and present reality, that he saw the Cross in the light of a perpetual Easter. For Easter is not only a historical event. The risen Christ is the living Christ who lives amongst us and within us. His grace is so sufficient that the cross He gives His Saints to bear can become glorious and 'perfect joy'.

(3) The third Crucifixion in Paul's Calvary is the Crucifixion of the world, which like the impenitent thief, died railing, and indeed died slowly. Paul was naturally a proud man, and though his consecration to our Lord was complete the death of the world in him was slow. He recalls not without pride I think, his Jewish ancestry and training: 'If any other man thinketh that he hath whereof he might trust in the flesh, I more.' But he tells us that the things that were gain to him he counted lost for Christ. He says indeed: 'I do count them but dung, that I may win Christ.' One cannot but feel in this and other passages, that there is some lingering pride left in him. We find, too, that the fact of his Roman citizenship was a matter of gratification to him. He was not unaffected by the glamour and glory of that great Roman world, and even in his Apologia in the Second Epistle to the Corinthians, though he glories in infirmities, one cannot but think that he was giving a true account of himself, when he said to the Philippians: 'Not as though I had already attained, either were already perfect.'[4]

The world dies slowly in us all. Spurts of rebellion sometimes frustrate even a Saint like the great Apostle. The prayer of St Paul is beautifully paraphrased in the words of Charles Wesley:

> Show me, as my soul can bear,
>   The depth of inbred sin;
> All the unbelief declare,
>   The pride that lurks within;
> Take me, whom Thyself hast bought,
>   Bring into captivity
> Every high aspiring thought
>   That would not stoop to Thee.

Most of the readers of this book, like the writer, have lived happy lives. Can we say, 'I have been crucified with Christ'? The essence of the Crucifixion of Jesus, is expressed in the words: 'Lo I come to do thy will.' Where there is a true consecration to Christ, even though we have had no great tribulations to

[4] Philippians 3:12.

rejoice in, there is at least some sense in which we can utter these words, which when we think of them may seem terrible and almost impossible to follow.

Have you ever asked yourself the question: 'Did Jesus want to be crucified?' The answer, I think, is certainly in the negative, otherwise there would be no meaning in the anguish of Gethsemane when Jesus said: 'If it be thy will, take this cup from me.' In the sense that Jesus bore the sorrows and sins of many—He was a man of Sorrows; but He was not a sorrowful man, and His normal life is perhaps more truly described in the words of the Epistle to the Hebrews: 'Thou hast anointed him with the oil of gladness above his fellows.'

The Gospel narrative shows us that Jesus loved feasting and took pleasure in the innocent joys of life. If tribulations are our lot, as they have been that of multitudes of people, even in our own day to the extent of martyrdom, then we have the assurance that the grace of Christ is sufficient for us. John Wesley said, and I am sure he was right, that God wishes His children to be happy, and indeed we miss the meaning of both St Paul and St Francis, unless we realize that they found joy in the Cross that Christ gave them to bear.

It is no part of my purpose to suggest that the Christian life is an easy one, but I think it is true that if our consecration to Christ is complete, we always find joy in doing His will, whatever comes to us, whether pleasure or suffering.

In the early Church we have two stories of martyrdoms with which many of us are familiar: the story of Polycarp and the story of Ignatius. There is a great difference in the attitude to martyrdom of these two men. Ignatius literally threw himself on death and begged people to do nothing to prevent his glory in martyrdom. He sought the wild beasts and found them. Polycarp was quite different; when he knew that martyrdom might come, he went to a farm to escape the Romans. When they arrested him and he saw that martyrdom was inevitable, though eighty-six years of age, he faced it with noble heroism and gloried in the Cross of Christ.

F

I cannot but think that Polycarp's was the right and Christian attitude toward martyrdom. As St Francis says, infirmities when they come are gifts of God. When we think of martyrdom and terrible tribulation, we tremble and fear that we should ever bear them. Perhaps we can get help from erring Peter. Who can forget those searching questions of the Saviour, 'Lovest thou me?', and the agony of Peter when he remembered his cowardly denial, perhaps fearful that such a denial might again occur. May we not at least repeat the words which he so passionately uttered, 'Thou knowest all things Lord, thou knowest that I love thee', and devote ourselves, whether in tribulation or in joy, to do the Will of God.

We do well to keep the Festival of the Holy Cross and ever to say:

> *Nothing in my hand I bring,*
> *Simply to Thy Cross I cling.*

CHAPTER EIGHT

MICHAELMAS

(29th September)

Epistle: Revelation 12[7].   *Gospel:* Matthew 18[1].

> *Lo to faith's enlightened sight,*
> *All the mountain flames with light*
> *Hell is nigh, but God is nigher,*
> *Circling us with hosts of fire.*

SOME remnants of the secular festivities of Michaelmas still linger amongst us, as readers of folk lore will recall; but what of the religious significance of this Festival? I acknowledge that I write this chapter with greater hesitation than any other in the book, and that, not because I disbelieve in angels, for both reason and Scripture make such a disbelief impossible. It would be difficult indeed to conclude that an almighty and all holy God had created no creatures higher than ourselves, and everywhere in Scripture the existence of angels is assumed even though it is not everywhere expressed. Notwithstanding, it is necessary to call to mind the words of St Paul to the Colossians: 'Let no man beguile you of your reward in a voluntary humility and worshipping of angels, intruding into those things which he hath not seen, vainly puffed up by his fleshly mind.'[1] Already gnostic teaching was beginning in Colossæ; and the doctrine that matter was evil and the fantastic theory of innumerable spiritual intermediaries between God and man was the most deadly error with which Christians had to contend. It challenged their belief in one Mediator between God and man, Jesus Christ, who was made Flesh and dwelt among us.

Although we are not in danger of falling into this error today, there is a sickly and sentimental form of angelology which we must avoid. Some minds seem to confuse angels and fairies, and the flimsy, winged creatures of sentimental piety differ

[1] Colossians 2[18].

greatly from the mighty angels of the Bible. I remember the shock that I received when witnessing the Passion Play at Oberammergau, through the almost pantomimic angel which appeared in the Garden of Gethsemane—the only thing in the whole play which seemed irreverent or trivial.

The exact meaning of the word 'angel' is messenger. It is sometimes difficult to know whether the term refers to a purely human messenger or a supernatural one. But perhaps it is better for us to think of the work of the angels than to define them. 'Are they not all ministering spirits, sent forth to minister for them who shall be heirs of salvation?'[2]

Angels are ministering spirits, not only to men, but to God. There are three outstanding things which the Scripture teaches about them: (a) their adoration of God, (b) their ministry of guardianship and help to men, (c) their militancy against the spiritual powers of Evil.

(a) Nowhere in Scripture is there so noble a description of the adoring Angels as in Isaiah's vision of the six-winged Seraphim worshipping God. Awe and reverence naturally spring to our minds when we read this vision of the great Prophet. God can only be perfectly worshipped by pure spirits who come before Him with deep reverence saying: 'Holy, Holy, Holy.' Isaiah, being a polluted man, is almost driven to despair by the thought of his own sinfulness. When a vision of God comes to us, can we do better than say:

> *How shall polluted mortals dare*
> *To sing Thy glory or Thy grace?*
> *Beneath Thy feet we lie afar,*
> *And see but shadows of Thy face.*

And yet is there a higher moment in spiritual experience than that in which we are permitted to say: 'Therefore with Angels and Archangels, we laud and magnify Thy glorious Name: ever more praising Thee, and saying, Holy, holy, holy . . .'?

We cannot understand the adoration of the Angels, but

[2] Hebrews 1[14].

through such a vision as that of Isaiah, we get a glimpse of things that 'Eye hath not seen, nor ear heard'. We must be content and thankful for the adoration of the angels and try to listen to

> *Angel voices, ever singing*
> *Round Thy throne of light,*
> *Angel harps, for ever ringing,*
> *Rest not day nor night;*
> *Thousands only live to bless Thee,*
> *And confess Thee*
> *Lord of Might.*

(*b*) How do the angels minister to the 'heirs of salvation'? Let us remember that no man in his normal, waking consciousness has ever seen a winged angel. Normally, spirits are in their nature invisible, but where they seem to have taken visible form, as sometimes the Bible indicates, there is no reason to think that the form was other than human. If the Gospel narratives of the resurrection are compared, we find that whereas in Matthew an angel is seen, in Mark it is 'a young man' in a white robe who is seen. Surely it is the man in white who is the angel, the messenger of God.

The wings of the Archangel Gabriel to be seen in many pictures are created by the artists' imagination. All the descriptions of winged angels, and there are many of them, which we find in holy Scripture, are from the pens of men who are describing trance, vision, or dream. The great fact about any dream is that it is symbolical in its structure, and it needs interpretation to be understood. Pharaoh and Nebuchadrezzar could not understand the symbolism of their dreams. They found interpreters in Joseph and Daniel. And a psychologist of today such as Dr Rivers, though he would give a different explanation of symbol from that of the Ancients, equally agrees with them that the 'stuff of which dreams are made' is figure and symbol. To treat symbolic metaphor literally, as has been so often done, is to misunderstand the truth it is intended to convey. That the scriptural language about angels is metaphorical can be illustrated by the fact of the change of metaphor. In Psalm 91 for instance, we find the metaphor of wings applied to the Almighty: 'He that dwelleth in the secret place of the most High, shall abide under the shadow of the Almighty. . . . He shall cover thee with his feathers and under his wings shalt thou trust. . . . For he shall give his angels charge over thee. . . . They shall bear thee up in their hands.'

Here, then, God is represented with wings and angels with hands. Since angels are the instruments of God in dealing with man, the figure of the hand is perhaps even more forceful than that of wings.

There is a legitimate use of the imagination which is not only found in Scriptural writers, but in poets and artists ever since. The sweet and perfect innocence of a pure spirit has never been more clearly demonstrated than in the angel faces which Fra Angelico imagined and pictured. Literal-minded Anglo-Saxons too often fail to realize the beauty and truth that imagination shapes in pictures and in words. Shakespeare tells us that the poet gives 'to airy nothing a local habitation and a name'. It is equally true, of course, of airy 'something'. The ethereal, the spiritual, the intangible, when treated by the poet or artist who try to give to such ethereal existences form and shape, do help blunter minds to see things that otherwise would have been hidden. The poets are telling the truth by means of their vision, and even by what sometimes we should call their fictions. We heavy-footed literalists should heed the warning of a modern poet who says: 'Tread softly . . . on my dreams.'

There are innumerable angels of God. In some sense all creation has angelic possibilities of adoration. Such hymns as the *Benedicite* and Psalm 148 call upon all created things to glorify God and magnify His name for ever. He makes clouds his ministers and flames of fire his angels.[3] Hence we need not be surprised when sun, moon and stars, daylight and night, winds and storms, whales and fishes, animals and birds, snow

[3] This seems to be the true translation of the Psalm quoted in Hebrews 1.

and frost, and many other creatures and things, are called upon to adore the Almighty:

> O all ye the Works of the Lord, bless ye the Lord:
> Praise him, and magnify him for ever.
> O ye Angels of the Lord, bless ye the Lord:
> Praise him, and magnify him for ever.

In our practical life, if we deal with angels, it is with spiritual and invisible beings who can only communicate with us as spirits: 'Spirit with spirit may meet.' And of such commerce can we be doubtful? Have not the dullest of us experiences of intuitions and admonitions which came we knew not whence? Have there not been moments of peril when a mystic voice has seemed to say: 'Go no farther'? and moments of cowardice when we have been prompted to go forward and dare?

It may be that such moments are rare to us, but a consciousness of spiritual guidance and guardianship is shared, so far as my experience goes, by multitudes of Christian people. God sends His help to us in innumerable ways. We are aware of movements in our hearts and thoughts, of strange intuitions which can only be explained in the terms of spiritual intercourse. Are we not also subject to such influences when we are unconscious of them? 'He giveth to His beloved in their sleep.'

(c) There are passages in Scripture—one a very notable one—in which the warfare, the long warfare between Good and Evil, is expressed in the terms of conflict—of the Conflict of Angelic Powers. St Paul says: 'We wrestle not against flesh and blood, but against principalities, against powers . . . in high places.'

This is a struggle which, he tells us, can only be carried on with spiritual weapons, we can only prevail as we have spiritual help. The reverence which the people had for the Archangel Michael was due to the regard in which he was held as the standard-bearer of God in the great warfare with the Evil One. We really have no plain account of the Archangel. He is a figure in the dreams of Daniel and in the visions of the Apocalypse. Probably in the Epistle of Jude the reference to him is a quotation from the Book of Enoch, that strange Apocalyptic writing. But of this we may be sure, that God has unseen forces of good, hosts to use in the battle between good and evil. 'The Lord of Hosts is with us.' There are secret hidden forces of evil in the world which we cannot understand, and which in our times have arisen like the Beast out of the Abyss; but we believe that God and His Hosts will conquer, and that Good is the final goal of ill.

Let us now ask what Jesus has to tell us about Angels. With the beautiful Gospel narrative of St Luke, where we read of the Angel of the Annunciation and the herald angels, I shall deal in Chapter 9 (St Luke's Day). Of the actual relation of Jesus to angels, we have some account. The outstanding fact is that He rejected their help. He would not trust in the help of angels, as Satan tempted Him to do, to uphold Him if He threw Himself down from the Temple height. More plainly, in His last Agony, though He said He might have had more than twelve legions of angels to help Him, He declined their help. Jesus, we are told, took not on Him the nature of angels, but the seed of Abraham. It was as man made like unto His brethren that He came into the world to save the world. He deliberately lived a human life and was straitened by the limitations of that life. He would ask from God no help in His life that one of His brethren could not receive. He gave to us the model of perfect manhood, the model for our imitation.

We are told that both in the temptation in the wilderness and in Gethsemane, angels came to help and comfort Him. What this means, we are not told, and it passes our comprehension; but it does seem improbable that such angels were other than invisible spiritual beings.

There can be no doubt that our Lord assumed the existence of angels. But He says very little about them. When the curious conundrum about marriage was given Him to answer, He said: 'For in the resurrection they neither marry, nor are given in marriage, but are as the angels of God in heaven'.[4]

4 Matthew 22²⁰.

Also he told us that when the Son of man comes again He will be accompanied by Holy Angels.

There are, however, two notable references to the angels which cannot be too often quoted; the former shows that the angels in Heaven are interested in the sinful people on earth and so we read: 'Likewise, I say unto you, there is joy in the presence of the angels of God over one sinner that repenteth' (see Luke 15$^{7-10}$). A charming paraphrase of these words is found in a hymn by Charles Wesley:

> *Ready for you the angels wait,*
> *To triumph in your blest estate;*
> *Tuning their harps, they long to praise*
> *The wonders of redeeming grace.*

The second passage is the one which of all sayings about angels in the New Testament seems to me the most illuminating and helpful:

'Take heed that ye despise not one of these little ones; for I say unto you, That in heaven their angels do always behold the face of my Father which is in heaven' (Matt 18^{10}).

In the Book of Revelation we read: 'The mystery of the seven stars which thou sawest in my right hand, and the seven golden candlesticks. The seven stars are the angels of the seven churches: and the seven candlesticks which thou sawest are the seven churches' (1^{20}).

These words are themselves an interpretation of St John's vision, but they have been understood in different ways. The meaning of them almost certainly is that the star, the Angel of the Church, is the ideal, and the candlestick—or better the lamp—with its dingy burning wick, is the actuality. But then the Lord Himself walks amongst the candlesticks and so keeps the lamps burning. With this picture in our minds of the bright-burning, ideal angel star and the poor imitation of the actual churches, we may turn to the eighteenth chapter of St Matthew's Gospel: It begins with the question: 'Who is the greatest in the kingdom of heaven?'—which Jesus answers by taking a little child and setting him in the midst of them, and going on to warn them in terrible words of the wickedness of putting stumbling-blocks in the way of the little ones. In conclusion He says to them: 'Take heed that ye despise not one of these little ones; for I say unto you, That in heaven their angels do always behold the face of my Father which is in heaven' (18[10]). Then His mood seems to change and we read the words: 'For the Son of man is come to save that which was lost.'

If these words are interpolated, as some think, the interpolation was a good one, because it is interpretative of the Matthean version of the parable of the lost sheep, which rather surprisingly in this context follows. The final words, 'Even so it is not the will of your Father which is in heaven, that one of these little ones should perish', evidently applied not to the innocent little child, but to the lost sheep. For of these it is also true that 'their angels do always behold the face of my Father which is in heaven'.

The truth is that Jesus came to save the least and the last, and they are all spoken of (both the innocent child and the guilty and strayed soul) as little ones whose angels (who as Swedenborg says, never grow old) always appear before the face of the Father in heaven. The angel that he sees is the ideal child created by Him and still before His eyes even when the actual child has strayed like the lost sheep.

The loving eyes of God see the human being as He meant him to be, however far, however much, his soul is marred and tarnished by sin. It is in such a way that Jesus looked upon the woman who was a sinner and saw the sinner who was a woman made in the image of God. It is a false proverb that says: 'Love is blind.' In reality, nothing sees so much or so well. God looks through the actual filth in many a human being and sees the ideal, the Angel which He made him to be.

Many years ago I visited a famous church and was very much impressed by the enthusiasm of the sexton who showed me round it and evidently loved every stick and stone of the building.

When I was examining the choir, he pointed out some panels and said to me: 'Can you see anything on them?'; and I said: 'Yes.' 'What can you see?' he asked. I replied: 'Dirt.' 'Look again, I will get a candle that you may see more clearly'; and he brought one that I might examine the panels in its light. He said: 'Do you see anything now?' I replied: 'Only dirt.' 'Oh,' he said, 'that is very curious. It is precisely what the vicar told me when I showed him these panels; but I got him to allow me to remove some of them and clean them. I will show you them. Follow me.' He took me into another part of the church and he showed me the panels he had taken down, and explained the process by which he had cleaned them. He had succeeded, with great patience, in removing the accumulated dirt of centuries. He was right, there was something to see; for on these panels were painted the faces of angels and saints. Only a year or two ago, I went back to that church and looked upon the angel faces upon those ancient panels now restored to their original place in the chancel. The critic could see nothing but dirt; the vicar—the official—was equally blind. But the man who loved every stick and stone of the place could see through the dirt. It is just so that the heavenly Father sees the angel in the most polluted men.

Perhaps I may be accused of falling into the snare of fancifulness, against which I have warned readers, but I would ask where do Faith, Hope, and Charity come from? They are not catalogued among the primary virtues of ancient morality. They are distinctive Christian virtues. Where do they come from? St John tells us that we love Him because He first loved us. Is there any sense in which we can say we believe in Him because He first believed in us, or we hope because He first hoped for us? Surely, Faith, Hope, and Love came down from Heaven, and though it may be but a fancy, I like to think of them as three Angels in the bosom of the heavenly Father. It is His Faith and His Hope and His Love that are at the base of man's salvation. He loves His children and sees the good in them. He hopes for them as the father with the prodigal son hoped for the return of the wayfarer, and He believes in man. It is the Devil who disbelieves in man, who says to God: 'Doth Job serve God for naught?' He is the great disbeliever. When nobody else believes in us, or loves us, or has any hope for us, when we no longer believe in ourselves and give up all hope of being the men and women God meant us to be, our angels are always before the face of our Father which is in heaven.

Many years ago I remember reading one of the dreams of Olive Schreiner. It was called the 'Dream of Wild Bees', and described a woman who was thinking of her unborn child. It was a hot day in South Africa, and a swarm of wild bees were humming and buzzing round about her, and as they hummed she became drowzy and fell asleep. A strange mental picture in her half-dreaming and half-waking state formed itself in her brain; the bees seemed to lengthen themselves out and become human creatures. One after another they came and spoke to her and said that if they could touch her side, the little one about to be born would be endowed with this or that gift. One said, 'I will give him health'; another, 'wealth'; another, 'fame'; but presently a more drab-looking one said: 'If I touch your side, I do not promise health, but there will wake up in the blood of the child a burning fever which will lick his blood as fire.' 'Do you give wealth?' she said. 'No, perhaps poverty.' 'Fame?' 'No, he may be in the eyes of men even infamous.' 'What then do you give?' 'The ideal shall be real to him.' And this was the gift that the mother chose. Is not this the greatest of all gifts? that the angel shall be realized, and that no man need despair because of his failures since his angel is always before the face of the Father which is in heaven?

And then there are those other angels there, those whose heart and mind are fixed upon the return of penitent sinners, and are already tuning their harps to join in that Hallelujah chorus which the angels in heaven in their joy sing, over one sinner that repenteth.

Angels of Jesus, angels of light,
Singing to welcome the pilgrims of the night!

CHAPTER NINE

ST LUKE THE EVANGELIST

(18th October)

Epistle: 2 Timothy 4¹¹.   *Gospel:* Luke 10¹.

Almighty God, who calledst Luke the Physician, whose praise is in the Gospel, to be an Evangelist, and Physician of the soul; May it please thee, that, by the wholesome medicines of the doctrine delivered by him, all the diseases of our souls may be healed; through the merits of thy Son Jesus Christ our Lord. Amen.

COLLECT OF THE DAY

'Only Luke is with me'

VERY little is known, the authorities tell us, about St Luke. This is true of his external life. Indeed, only two biographical details to which credit can be given have been preserved by Eusebius, the fourth-century historian: That he was born at Antioch and martyred at Petras. Other traditions are speculative or legendary. But is it true to say that we know little about St Luke? Great authors live in their writings. The little we know about Shakespeare is much less in value for real knowledge of him than his plays. The writings of St Luke do actually give us much knowledge of the man.

THE ARTIST

One thing is quite clear—Luke was an artist. The tradition that he was a painter who portrayed in colours the Mother of Jesus is generally regarded today to be an incredible legend; but it is true that he has given us an incomparable word-portrait of the Blessed Virgin, which is much the most complete picture we have of her.

Familiar stories, which we read repeatedly, sometimes spring into life as we re-read them. Such an experience was mine when for the hundredth or more time I read the story of the Nativity in St Luke's Gospel at Christmas. The sheer beauty of the story came home to me with new force. The extraordinary artistic skill of St Luke can hardly be better illustrated than by his Nativity stories. The account of the birth of John the Baptist, the story of the Annunciation and the Visitation, and of the shepherds watching their flocks at night, must be admitted to be, even as literature, amongst the most beautiful stories ever told. The skill and arrangement of the material of these narratives is the work of a great artist. The pictures which he drew in words have inspired the great painters of the world to produce many masterpieces of art. That St Luke, the careful historian, got his knowledge of the facts from the Mother of Jesus herself seems to me almost certain. His own declaration in the preface of his Gospel, of the eye-witnesses who had supplied him with information are a confirmation of this claim. To her information St Luke no doubt gave artistic form.

One fact about ancient historians must always be kept in mind. When they recorded the speeches of their heroes, they made no special attempt to give verbatim reports; but often put into literary form the thoughts of the men of whom they wrote. To some degree this may be true of some of the hymns, for instance, of the Nativity narratives. It is difficult to see how the hymn of Zacharias—the *Benedictus*—could have been known in detail by St Luke, although he would be well aware of the sentiments and some of the phrases expressed in it. This would be less true of the *Magnificat*, because that extraordinary outpouring of thanksgiving to God by the lowly Maid, and the wonder and glory of God's uplifting of the humble and poor, must have been a theme over which Mary pondered often, though it is not impossible that Luke, to some extent, shaped its literary form. I like to think that the beautiful fancy of Botticelli in his picture 'The Madonna of the *Magnificat*' is true, and that when she was nursing the Infant Jesus, she may well have called to mind her great hymn and with her own pen wrote it down for the lovely angel children of the picture to sing. And I can well imagine that she sings it still. . . .

It must have been from Mary that St Luke heard the story

of the Shepherds. She would tell him what they told her, and he I think, gave inimitable shape to the story, interpreting for us all the great light which the Shepherds saw, and preserving for all times the Angelic message of Peace on earth to men of good will.

Many instances could be quoted from his gospel of his artistic skill and the beauty of his narrative. He had the gift in a remarkable degree of succinct statement which never ignored the picturesque detail—a rare combination in a literary artist. Can anything more picturesque or succinct be imagined than the beautifully told story of the woman who was a sinner, in the house of the Pharisee? One other instance of his artistry is the post Resurrection story of the walk of Jesus to Emmaus. Many people think that this is the most beautifully told story in the Gospel. How readily we picture those two disconsolate men with blinded eyes as they are overtaken by that unrecognized companion, who interprets to them the Scriptures with such thrilling force that they invite him to come and stay with them. How significant the revelation that opens their eyes as they recognize a familiar gesture when Jesus breaks the bread, and find the reason for their own burning hearts and a joy unspeakable. The beauty of this narrative is a triumph of artistic grace and subtle skill.

In the Acts of the Apostles the eye-witness narratives of St Luke are not less remarkable. His detailed account of the storm-tossed vessel in the Mediterranean has a graphic character which surprises even nautical men by its accuracy. It is often claimed that the story of this voyage is the best travel-story of ancient writers. It is not difficult to establish the claim that St Luke was an artist.

THE HISTORIAN

It is an interesting fact that Professor Ramsay, who undertook his great works on St Paul, not primarily as a theologian, but as a lay scholar interested in classical antiquity, came to the conclusion unexpectedly that St Luke was one of the greatest historians of antiquity. His illuminating writing is based on that conclusion.

The Acts of the Apostles is no mere chronicle of events, but a carefully designed work, artistic as well as historic. Some years ago an interesting theory was propounded by Dr Ironside Still, under the title of *St Paul on Trial*. Dr Still argues that the Acts of the Apostles, though an account of the development of early Christianity, was primarily a brief written for perusal by Paul's distinguished friend Theophilus, as a defence of the Apostle at the Court of Cæsar. This theory, though it has much to be said for it, has not been widely accepted by scholars, but Dr Still's analysis of the book proves that it was a carefully designed work of historical art. In it, St Luke writes both as a collector of events that happened before he himself became a Christian, and in the last half of the book as an eye-witness of what he himself actually saw. When he was not actually present, he was able immediately to get necessary information from those who were.

One evidence of design is to be found in Dr Still's numbering of the first seven sections of the book. He points out that the work in each section is expressed by a clause such as that which concludes the first section: 'And the Lord added to them day by day those that were being saved.' Similar endings of all the other sections enable us to realize the gradual expansion of early Christianity.[1]

Whether the book was written, as Dr Still suggests, as a brief for the defence of St Paul may be doubtful; but it is quite clear that St Paul was the hero of the historian, and the chief agent in the evangelization of the Gentiles and their reception into the Christian Church. St Luke does seem to have the defence of the greatly criticized St Paul in his mind when he writes this book. It is very significant that the records of expanding Christianity are given in such a way as to show that Paul's Gentile mission was no innovation in the Church. The Jerusalem Church had already sanctioned the admission of the heathen before Paul

[1] See Acts 2^{47}, 5^{14-16}, 6^7, 9^{31}, 12^{24}, 16^5, 19^{20}.

began his mission. Nothing is recounted with more emphasis than St Peter's baptism of Cornelius. In fact it is noticeable that Luke thinks it so important that he tells the story of Peter's vision twice.

Peter's deliverance from narrow-minded Judaism is a remarkable fact and there are few sayings more notable than his statement: 'Of a truth I perceive that God is no respecter of persons: but in every nation he that feareth him, and worketh righteousness, is accepted with him' (Acts 10[34-5]).

Not only is the baptism of Cornelius to be noted, but the gradual expansion of the Church among the Samaritans, with whom the Jews had no dealings, and the baptism of the Ethiopian Eunuch by Philip. These incidents clearly show the expansion of Christianity amongst non-Jewish people before the great mission of Paul and Barnabas was undertaken. The expanding character of the Church is emphasized in the endings of the sections which have already been noted.

With such a beginning St Luke shows that the great missionary work of Paul in Asia Minor and Europe could not be objected to on the nationalistic ground which was so often urged against the great Apostle by his enemies. The story of the mission of St Paul is told with great skill, and finds its climax when St Paul after much trouble reaches Rome, the Metropolis itself, and is left there, though a prisoner, still preaching the Gospel.

The story of St Paul as told by St Luke is one of magnificent heroism and suffering for the cause of Christ, but also of a victorious campaign which ultimately issued in the conversion of the whole Roman Empire to Christianity.

I remember reading in the work of a German critic of Christianity that he could find no similarity between the Paul of St Luke and the Paul of the Epistles. It would be difficult indeed to discover a more prejudiced statement than this. The man whom Luke describes in his exterior mission is identical in character with the man self-revealed in Paul's letters. The same vehemence and passion, mingled with competency, is to be found in Luke's history and Paul's letters. My space

G

prevents further treatment of this subject, but it is well worth study. St Luke shows himself in the Acts of the Apostles not only to be a great historian, but a great biographer.

SYNOPTIST AND INTERPRETER

When we speak of St Luke as an Evangelist, our first impulse is to think of him as the writer of one of the Synoptic Gospels, and it is true no doubt that the bulk of his writing is the same in substance as that of Mark and Matthew. But I want to dwell upon those aspects of St Luke which were individual and personal rather than those which he had in common with the other writers of the Gospel. While the value of his confirmation of what the others say is obvious, there is a difference in outlook and approach which cannot be ignored.

There can be little doubt that St Luke used St Mark's Gospel, that he also had access to other manuscripts in common with St Matthew, and that he seems to have known of records, though it cannot be quite certain whether these were written or spoken, which St Matthew did not know; and it is agreed that St Matthew also had records, probably unknown to, and certainly unused by St Luke. It is interesting and instructive to notice any differences of expression in the material common to both of them. The instance of the Sermon on the Mount will come to everyone's mind. St Matthew makes one discourse of what St Luke treats in a more fragmentary fashion. The tendency here and elsewhere in St Luke to emphasize our Lord's love of the poor is a notable one. Careful comparisons of such distinctions are instructive and helpful to the student of the Gospels.

St Luke evidently gave considerable thought to sayings of Jesus which were not at first clear to him. His value as an interpreter of such sayings should not be overlooked. The principal instance is his account of the Transfiguration, of which I have already written; it gives the only explanation of the reason of our Lord's journey to Mount Hermon. But why was it that St Luke in his record of our Lord's sayings about prayer, which are practically identical with those of St Matthew, should have made one striking exception and have said, not (like St Matthew) that the heavenly Father would give good gifts to them who asked Him, but that He would give the Holy Spirit to them who asked Him. It may be of course, that Jesus said both these things at different times; but it is more likely that both evangelists were dealing with the same manuscript, and if so the change seems rather strange. Is it possible that the explanation is that St Luke realized that the gifts of the heavenly Father were of little use to people unless they received them? The world is full of God's gifts, but many people fail to see that they are there. Did Luke write these words because he realized that a spirit of perceptivity and receptivity were necessary for the reception of the heavenly Father's gifts?

Another instance of his interpretation is to be found in his record of our Lord's sayings about loving our enemies. There is no substantial difference between the accounts given of these sayings in the record of the two Evangelists, except in the application. St Matthew represents Jesus as saying: 'Be ye therefore perfect, even as your Father which is in heaven is perfect.' St Luke's record, however, is different. He says: 'Be ye therefore merciful, as your Father also is merciful.' Does not the version of St Luke more perfectly represent the meaning of Jesus? It is evidently impossible for anyone to be perfect as God is. We cannot be omniscient or omnipresent. The only perfection we are capable of is perfection in love. The man who is merciful as God is merciful is as perfect as a man can be. Christian perfection is perfection in love. St Paul echoes Luke exactly when he says: 'Be ye therefore followers of God as dear children; and walk in love.' Do not St Luke's words suggest a deliberate interpretation of a saying that could easily be misunderstood? The interpretative value of such differences is worthy of note.

EVANGELIST

We are all familiar with St Paul's description of Luke as the 'beloved physician'. Harnack, who used St Paul's words as the title of his well-known book writes that 'distinct traces of medical diagnosis and scientific knowledge' are found in Luke's writings, and that 'the language even where questions of medicine or of healing are not touched upon, is coloured by medical phraseology; and in those passages where the author speaks as an eye-witness medical traits are especially and prominently apparent'. The evidence which strongly supports the ancient tradition that Luke was a medical man is unquestionably valuable, but a greater value for our understanding of St Luke is the description of him in the Collect of the Day as one 'whose praise is in the Gospel' as an 'evangelist and physician of the soul'.

The word evangelist as applied to St Luke means much more than the writer of a Synoptic Gospel. Apart from the Gospel of St Luke, our knowledge of Jesus as the Saviour of all men, and as the Saviour of individual men would be restricted in such a way that the Gospel would be greatly impoverished. Nearly all the records in the Gospel of our Lord's Saviourhood of individuals are to be found in St Luke, and the realization of His redeeming mission of mankind is much more clearly and un-ambiguously taught in this Gospel than in the other Synoptics. I do not mean by this that St Matthew and St Mark did not believe that Jesus was the Saviour of mankind; but I do mean that we should lack instances of His work during His lifetime as the Saviour of Souls, were it not for St Luke's record. Some-one may perhaps note that the saying of Jesus, that the Son of Man gave His life a ransom for many, is only to be found in Mark and Matthew; but it must not be forgotten that this saying was given to His disciples as an instance of the way in which they should sacrifice themselves for the sake of others.

It is also true of course that the great invitation of Jesus to those who labour and are heavy laden, is only to be found in St Matthew's Gospel. But the interpretation of these words as an invitation to all sinful men comes from reading into the saying the teachings of St Luke. The words were not originally spoken to sinners as such, but to people who were trying to be

good by laborious and fruitless methods. In the English Communion office, the translation of the Great Bible is preserved:
'Come unto me all that travail and are heavy laden,' it says,
'and I will refresh you.' It is notable that that great modern
translator of the Bible (Dr Moffatt) should also have used the
word 'refresh' instead of 'give you rest'. While it is quite true
that these words can be appropriately applied to all sinful people,
it is St Luke's Gospel of Salvation for sinful men which legitima-
tizes this application of them.

The modern Evangelist who preaches from Matthew and
Mark little realizes how greatly he interprets their words by
St Luke's Gospel.

Generally speaking, we may say that St Matthew is writing
for good people or people who are trying to be good, whereas
St Luke always has in mind the disreputable outcast whom
Jesus came to save. This of course is no disparagement of St
Matthew's Gospel. His message was needed as well as St Luke's.
But it is in St Luke, and I think only in St Luke, that Jesus is
vividly represented, not only as the Healer of the sick but as the
great Physician of the sinful. It is true that St Matthew tells us
that Jesus came to call sinners and not the righteous to repentance
and that He is the friend of publicans and sinners, but only
St Luke gives instances of the way in which He sought lost souls.
The Collect for the day gives thanks for St Luke as an evangelist
and physician of the soul. This is his distinctive mission. Have
we ever realized how utterly dependent we are on St Luke for
stories of what we should call the evangelical activities of our
Saviour? What parallel can we find in the other Gospels to such
narratives as the forgiveness of the sinful woman in the house of
Simon the Pharisee, or to the way in which Jesus sought and
saved the lost when He found in Zacchæus a soul when no one
else had ever thought of anything in this publican but an ill-
filled pocket? Is it often realized that the beautiful story of the
penitent thief is only told by St Luke? It is St Luke alone who
tells the parable of the Pharisee and the publican and he alone
records the parable of the lost coin. And the greatest of all the

parables of Jesus, the parable of the prodigal son, which has been well called the gospel within the Gospel, would be unknown to us if Luke had not recorded it.

The obligations of simple men to St Luke are so great that there is no Festival Day which we can keep with more thankfulness than that of St Luke the Evangelist.

It is notable too that St Luke, unlike St Matthew, does not record the saying of Jesus, that His Mission is confined to the house of Israel. It is perhaps natural that St Luke the Gentile, fellow of St Paul in his missionary work, should be less interested in our Lord's mission to the Jews than to all mankind. Jesus the Saviour and the work of universal redemption is central to Luke's thinking. He alone makes record of the Lord's joy when the seventy, of whom alone Luke tells us, returned exhilarated by the success of their mission. How glad we are that St Luke records that sudden vision of Jesus: 'I beheld Satan as lightning fall from heaven.' The defeat of evil can be assured if all simple men like the seventy bear their witness to the Saviour.

THE GOOD COMPANION

In the Epistle for the Day, we read the words of St Paul: 'Only Luke is with me.' Other people might leave him, but St Luke never. How great the privilege must have been to have had the constant companionship of this faithful man.

Of all the criminals of whom I have heard in my lifetime, perhaps none so shocked and disgusted respectable people as Oscar Wilde. When he was in prison he wrote his book *De Profundis*, a book of deep penitence, in which he tells how he read again St Luke's Gospel, which he, no mean word-painter himself, calls the most beautiful book in the world. He found comfort in it.

I remember well when speaking to a ministerial friend of mine of the beauty of *De Profundis* as a really religious book, he said contemptuously: 'Just one more pose of this famous *poseur*; I do not want to read anything he says, the filthy beast!' Well,

I wonder? Repulsive as his unnatural crime was, is it not a test of evangelical faith that we should believe that Christ can save the foulest of sinners. Anyone who does not believe in the possibility of the salvation of an Oscar Wilde entirely fails to understand the greatness of God's mercy. If only Luke was with him in the prison even an Oscar Wilde would not lack in hope. When one reads of the love of Jesus to the foulest men and women, in the inimitable stories recorded in St Luke, the unworthiest of us discover a new hope for ourselves, and can sing with renewed faith:

> *The dying thief rejoiced to see*
> *That fountain in his day;*
> *And there may I, though vile as he,*
> *Wash all my sins away.*

CHAPTER TEN

ALL SAINTS' DAY

(1st November)

Epistle: Revelation 7².   *Gospel:* Matthew 5¹.

'O Almighty God, who hast knit together thine elect in one communion and fellowship, in the mystical body of thy Son Christ our Lord; Grant us grace so to follow thy blessed Saints in all virtuous and godly living, that we may come to those unspeakable joys, which thou hast prepared for them that unfeignedly love thee; through Jesus Christ our Lord.'

> *For all the saints who from their labours rest,*
> *Who Thee by faith before the world confessed,*
> *Thy name, O Jesu, be for ever blest. Alleluia!*

'Wherefore seeing we also are compassed about with so great a cloud of witnesses, let us lay aside every weight, and the sin which doth so easily beset us, and let us run with patience the race that is set before us, looking unto Jesus the author and finisher of our faith; who for the joy that was set before him endured the cross, despising the shame, and is set down at the right hand of the throne of God.'

CHRISTIAN people who have a race to run and a battle to fight are compassed about with a great cloud of witnesses, the Saints of God, who have run their race and have been victorious in their struggle with the foes of the spirit.

It is necessary in order to profit by the encouragement of these words to visualize the scene which was in the mind of the writer of them. He was thinking of the Roman Stadium, of the arena in which the sports of the day took place—the races, the wrestling-bouts, and sometimes, alas, the gladiatorial shows. Surrounding the arena were tiers of seats as one can see for instance in the Colosseum of Rome. The occupants of these seats are the great cloud of witnesses by which we are compassed about.

By a freak of language, the English word 'witness' can be applied to their onlooking, but that is not the meaning of the Greek original. Whilst they could not be other than onlookers, the word translated 'witnesses' really means 'those who bear witness.' We use the word in this other sense in connexion with the law courts. The ones who compass us about are those whose lives bear witness to the victory of Faith in God and the City of God. The passage is a summary and an application of what has been written in the preceding chapter, which is really an eloquent account of the men of faith who were the true heroes of the Hebrew nation.

Other historians, when they write of a nation's heroes, glory in their statesmanship, military skill, literary achievements, but the writer of the 11th Chapter of Hebrews, although he speaks of the soldiers and statesmen of the Hebrew race, does not glory in their skill, but in the fact that they were men of faith. Faith in God and the City of God was the characteristic which gave distinction to Hebrew history. The great cloud of witnesses, after defeat on earth, were now victors who encouraged their successors as they looked on their struggles to persevere in the race and conflicts of faith.

A notable fact is that none of the heroes of the Hebrew race was successful; they all failed to receive the promise. They sought the City of God but did not find it. And yet, 'God was not ashamed of them to be called their God.' God is not ashamed of the men who try and fail, but of the men who do not try. The quest for the City of God, of which the writer gives so eloquent an account, never ceases. It begins with Abraham, who though he sought a city with foundations, when he left his native city of Ur and 'followed the gleam', was fated only to dwell in moving tents. He failed to find the city, but he passed on the quest to his son Isaac, who in his turn passed it on to Jacob; and Jacob when he was dying 'blessed both the sons of Joseph, and worshipped, leaning upon the top of his staff'. And Joseph, a dreamer to the last, so believed in the city of God that he visualized an event four hundred years after when the Israelites would leave Egypt, and 'gave commandment concerning his bones'. This evidently means that even when dead, he hoped to lead the Israelitish people to the Promised Land.

When under Joshua they entered the land of Promise, and even afterwards when each man could sit under his own 'vine and fig tree', they were like mountain climbers, who discover when they reach their immediate objective, that the mountain summit still towers above them. So the prophets of Israel, not satisfied with the material city which their people inhabited, kept continually before their eyes the ideal City of God.

The history of Israel is the history both of a failure to reach that city and a persistent faith which never wavered, notwithstanding defeat and exile, in its pursuit. And the quest has continued in the new Israel for twenty centuries. Men of faith still struggle on, and however baffled, believe that the kingdoms of this world shall become the kingdom of our God and His Christ. In that struggle men of faith are still engaged, but however long it takes, this faith is a victory that overcomes the world.

'Compassed about with a great cloud of witnesses.' Today we see in the surrounding seats, not only the men of faith of the Israelitish people, but the men who throughout the Christian era have continued the struggle. As we view these onlookers, we think of the twelve apostles, of their faith often to martyrdom, of the great Apostle of the Gentiles, St Paul, of heroes and martyrs of every generation. Cannot we see on those crowded seats the aged martyr, Polycarp; St Ambrose, St Augustine, Francis of Assisi, Bernard of Clairvaux, Hugh of Lincoln, Richard of Chichester; an innumerable company of saints and heroes of later times, often mistaken but never losing their faith in God and His city; Thomas More, possibly talking loud to Hugh Latymer, John and Charles Wesley in loving converse with Francis de Sales, or General Booth sitting quite near to Cardinal Newman. So we try to picture that great cloud of witnesses. Most of all perhaps, we think of those humble and simple people of whom 'Time fails us to tell', who by their simple faith have carried the burden of the Church upon their shoulders more constantly and unwaveringly even than the hierarchies; and we look for the dear faces of those whom we loved long since and lost awhile.

What do these onlookers, this great cloud of witnesses mean to us? It is true of course that:

> Only the actions of the just
> Smell sweet, and blossom in their dust

Certainly they stir us to admiration of their deeds and a desire to be like them, and we can join with George Eliot and express the wish:

> Oh may I join the choir invisible
> Of those immortal dead who live again
> In mind made better by their presence.

But George Eliot was a secularist. Is it true to think of the great cloud of witnesses as dead? As living only in the influence that the record of their lives has upon others? Are they nothing to us but mere exemplars of noble life? Does a Christian man mean nothing when he says, 'I believe in the Communion of Saints'? Has the cloud of witnesses no interest in the strugglers in the arena on which they look? Do Christian men really think that their loved ones, parents, helpers, friends, forget all about them when they sit in those tiers of seats looking on?

I cannot but think that the author of these inspiring words, interested as he was in the sports and the sports-ground of his day would have used a slightly different figure if he had been a modern Englishman. The natural figure for him to have used, would have been an English football or cricket ground. I have often wondered whether Francis Thompson was thinking of this passage when he wrote his delightful little poem: 'At Lord's.'

One of the great interests of that strange man's life was the game of cricket. He was an enthusiastic follower of the matches of his native county Lancashire, which explained his reference to the red roses in the caps of the Lancashire cricketers:

> It is little I repair to the matches of the Southron folk,
> Though my own red roses there may blow;
> It is little I repair to the matches of the Southron folk,
> Though the red roses crest the caps, I know.
> For the field is full of shades as I near the shadowy coast,
> And a ghostly batsman plays to the bowling of a ghost,
> And I look through my tears on a soundless-clapping host
> As the run-stealers flicker to and fro,
> To and fro;—
> O my Hornby and my Barlow long ago!

Is not that 'soundless clapping host' reminiscent of the great cloud of witnesses with which we are compassed about? I do not write either as a Roman Catholic or a Spiritualist, but do believe in the Communion of Saints.

Years ago I heard a story which was told me by a person whose word I have no reason to doubt, though I am quite unable to verify the facts. A famous cricketer, he told me, of the nineteenth century became blind, but his son gave promise of being even a greater cricketer than he. When at the university, he was selected to play in a great national match—I forget which. But before the day of the match his father died, and it was generally thought that he would not play. To the surprise of his friends, he not only played, but made a brilliant century. And indeed had probably never played so well before. When he returned to the pavilion, the crowd applauding him vociferously, a friend said: 'How could you play like that with your father lying dead at home?' His reply was: 'That is just the reason I played so well. My poor blind father always wanted to see me play, but this is the first day that it was possible.' He was right, the eyes of the blind are opened. Those who pass into the other life are able to see.

The Church of God, militant and triumphant, is one. No words describe this oneness more graphically than those of Charles Wesley:

> *Come, let us join our friends above*
> *That have obtained the prize,*
> *And on the eagle wings of love*
> *To joys celestial rise:*
> *Let all the saints terrestrial sing,*
> *With those to glory gone;*
> *For all the servants of our King,*
> *In earth and heaven, are one.*
>
> *One family we dwell in Him,*
> *One Church, above, beneath,*
> *Though now divided by the stream,*

The narrow stream of death:
One army of the living God,
To His command we bow;
Part of His host have crossed the flood,
And part are crossing now.

'The narrow stream of death'—what a narrow ditch it is!

The words 'We are compassed about with so great a cloud of witnesses' are written for our encouragement in the race we have to run. Our work is to run and wrestle, not to be on-lookers. No man has a right to be an onlooker in the battle of life, until he finds his way into the grand-stand, the only portal to which is death. Inactive Christians, and there are many of them, mere loiterers on the sports field, who instead of working —'For the night cometh when no man can work'—often impede by their careless indolence, the work of the Church. God calls us all to run the race that is set before us and to run it with patience—a better translation would be endurance or steadiness —laying aside every weight, and looking to Jesus, the author and perfector of our faith, as He was of the faith of the great cloud of witnesses.

Can we not put the exhortation of the writer into three words: strip, be steady, look.

(*a*) *Strip.* The Christian race is a serious undertaking. Years ago I attended the Sports of a famous school. The boys wore, when juniors, Eton jackets and silk hats; and the senior boys wore morning coats, and could often be seen on the streets of London with carelessly folded umbrellas in their hands. The Sports consisted of the ordinary foot races of events of that sort, and the racers wore garments as light as possible. But there was an amusing comic race of the 'old boys'; and for this, these young men wore their morning coats and their silk hats, and carried umbrellas in their hands. It was a comic spectacle to see these perspiring men, their coat-tails flapping, and their hats falling from their heads to be trampled on by the other runners. The whole spectacle caused much amusement to the onlookers.

But what was noticeable was the fact that these young men took more time, notwithstanding their strength and maturity, than the little boys who were stripped for the race.

The Christian race is not comic. Every weight must be laid aside, entangling sins left, as St Paul says, behind. How comic the race of many Christians seems, and how ineffective the race is when men try to carry with them as much worldly impedimenta as will permit them to scrape into heaven! This is a serious race, and the exhortation to lay aside every weight and the sin which doth so easily beset us is of imperative importance to those who run to win.

(b) *Be steady*. An important qualification for a successful Christian race is steadiness. It is not by certain spurts that the race is to be won, because it is a long race. Everyone knows the old fable of the hare and the tortoise. I remember as a boy how much annoyance it gave me that the slow, lumbering tortoise beat the agile hare. But life teaches us all this lesson.

If one may change the figure and compare the race to a march, Kipling's account of the march of the Roman soldiers in the South of England to the Roman wall may well be quoted: 'Rome's Race—Rome's Pace, as the proverb says. Twenty-four miles in eight hours, neither more nor less. Head and spear up, shield on your back, cuirass-collar open one hand's breadth—and that's how you take the Eagles through Britain.'

Nothing is more important to the soldiers of Christ than the daily performance of regular prayer and steady duty.

(c) *Look*. But perhaps most of all, the exhortation to keep one's eyes fixed on the goal, on Jesus the author and perfector of Faith, is the most important counsel of the three. The secret of the Saints of God has been the concentration of their minds and thoughts upon Jesus Himself. He is the central figure in the cloud of witnesses. He is of all men the one who 'never turned his back but marched breast forward'. His face was always turned to Jerusalem. The Christian is always in peril when his mind is deflected from Jesus. Though St Paul's words have no primary application to a race, they can be well applied to the heavenly race. But we all, with open face beholding as in a glass the glory of the Lord, are changed into the same image from glory to glory, even as by the Spirit of the Lord.'

The goal of all Christian striving is to be like Jesus, and to this end our gaze must be concentrated on Him.

> *Jesus, the First and Last,*
> *On Thee my soul is cast:*
> *Thou didst Thy work begin*
> *By blotting out my sin;*
> *Thou wilt the root remove,*
> *And perfect me in love.*
>
> *Yet when the work is done,*
> *The work is but begun:*
> *Partaker of Thy grace,*
> *I long to see Thy face;*
> *The first I prove below,*
> *The last I die to know.*

The Christian race is only one of the figures used by the writer as an illustration of the Christian life. Wrestling-bouts as well as foot-races took place in the arena of the Greek stadium and the figure of conflict is as important as that of racing. So we read: 'Ye have not yet resisted unto blood, striving against sin.' This, too, emphasizes the grim seriousness of the Christian life. When we think of the Christian duty of seeking first the Kingdom of God and His righteousness, and call to mind the long struggle of the great cloud of witnesses to build up the city of God, and their final victory after many defeats, we cannot but be thankful for the encouragement given to us by the Saints of God:

> *O blest communion, fellowship divine!*
> *We feebly struggle; they in glory shine,*
> *Yet all are one in Thee, for all are Thine.*

With such encouragement let us march:

> *On, to the bound of the waste,*
> *On, to the City of God.*

CHAPTER ELEVEN

ST HUGH OF LINCOLN

(17th November)

Epistle: Wisdom 10⁹.   *Gospel:* Mark 11²².

'*The shadow of a great rock in a weary land.*'

O merciful Father, who didst endue Thy servant with a wise and
cheerful boldness, and didst teach him how to commend the discipline
of holy life to kings and princes, give us grace not only to be bold,
but to have just cause for boldness, even the fear and love of Thyself
alone. Grant this, O Father, for the sake of Thy dear Son, our Lord and
Saviour, Jesus Christ.

COLLECT OF THE DAY

> *O most merciful Redeemer, Friend, Brother;*
> *May we know Thee more clearly,*
> *Love Thee more dearly,*
> *Follow Thee more nearly,*
> *Day by day. Amen.*

ST RICHARD (c. 1196–1253)

WHEN the Anglican authorities revised the calendar, they
omitted the Commemoration Days of the medieval
Saints, but with two notable exceptions, those of St. Richard of
Chichester and St Hugh of Lincoln. The holy characters and
self-sacrificing lives of these two men, rather than the alleged
miracles wrought by their relics, give them a high place amongst
the Saints. The beautiful prayer of St Richard of Chichester
printed at the head of this chapter is not only a legacy to the
Church of God, but a clue to the character of the man who
wrote it.

St Hugh of Lincoln is fortunate in his biographer, the Abbot
Adam, to whose integrity and honesty J. A. Froude gives a
striking testimony in his fascinating essay, 'A Bishop of the
Twelfth Century'.[1]

[1] Froude's *Short Studies*, Second series (Longmans, 1871).

Readers of the monkish chronicles of the Saints generally find a single pattern. The wonders and miracles attributed to most of them are of the same type, with the consequence that the individuality of the man of whom they are writing is greatly obscured; the halo is more conspicuous than the man. This, however, is not the case in Abbot Adam's biography of St Hugh, whose secretary he had been before he became an Abbot. A genuine man, whose lineaments we can clearly discern, is pictured by him. St Hugh is characterized by Froude in the following words: 'In the Hugo of Avalon with whom we are now to become acquainted we shall see nothing but the sunniest cheerfulness, strong masculine sense, inflexible purpose, up-rightness in word and deed; with an ever-flowing stream of genial and buoyant humour.'

In this chapter I shall gather from Froude's essay incidents in the life of St Hugh and some of his notable sayings, to illustrate the truth of the characterization which I have just quoted.

St Hugh, who is perhaps more truly described as Hugh of Avalon, was not an Englishman. He was born in the mountain-ous country near Grenoble on the borders of Savoy. His father was a nobleman. When he was eight years old, his mother died. This calamity so affected his father that he divided his inheritance between his two elder sons, and entered a monastery where he afterwards became a monk. He took the little Hugh with him, and he received his education in the college of the monastery. From the first, Hugh was designed for a religious life; but when he grew up, he was not content with the relatively easy life—though we should find it severe enough today—of the monastery in which his father had been a monk. He was attracted by the stern, terrible discipline of the Carthusian order in the near-by Grande Chartreuse. Like the noble youths of all time, he aspired after the hard and difficult things of life. His spirit was not dissimilar from that of young men who face the hardship of Polar expeditions or Himalayan heights. Notwithstanding the advice of a kindly old monk, the young Hugh determined to give the 'utmost for the highest'. This meant that he chose to be the fellow of men who were as hard as rocks; the old monk described them as men who had no mercy on their own bodies and none on others, and whose dress scraped the flesh from their bones. He added: 'The discipline will tear the bones themselves out of such frail limbs as yours.'

The discipline of the Order seems to us quite merciless. His food was most meagre, and 'his bedding was a horse-cloth, a pillow, and a skin. His dress was a horse-hair shirt covered outside with linen, which was worn night and day, and the white cloak of the order, generally a sheepskin and unlined—all else was bare.'

Hugh underwent this discipline and so far from succumbing to it, prevailed over its hardships. He became so accustomed to the solitary and disciplined life that in future days, when a high-placed dignity of Church and State, it was a positive relief to him to go back to his cell, and to put on his sheepskin, Froude says, 'as a modern man puts on his shooting jacket'.

Though hard to himself, Hugh disapproved of the merciless severity of some of the monks to their brethren when disobedient. He pointed out that God Himself, when He expelled our first parents from the garden of Eden, at least gave them a coat of skins. 'God', he said, 'tempers his anger with compassion. Man knows not what mercy means.'

In the collect of the day we read of the wise and cheerful boldness of the Saint, and of his learning how to commend the discipline of holy life to kings and princes. Who then were the kings and princes to whom he commended the discipline of holy life? They were Henry II, Richard I, and John, of England.

Henry II, who seems to have been really penitent for the murder of Thomas à Becket, decided, possibly as part of his penance, to introduce the Carthusian Order into England. A few of the brothers came, but their mission was unsuccessful, because no proper arrangements had been made to deal with the tenants on the Royal Estate which Henry gave to the Order. The first prior resigned and the second died. The remaining brothers of the community, in disgust, were about to return to the Grande Chartreuse, when Hugh, the outstanding monk of the Order, reluctantly came to England to take charge. He found everything in confusion, and bad blood and discontent on all hands. He came to the conclusion that the mission could not be successful unless the tenants of the Crown were treated with complete justice. Hence he went to the king and persuaded him to offer the tenants either entire enfranchisement, or farms of equal value on any other of the royal manors to be selected by themselves, and also to give them liberal compensation for the building and furnishing of their new homes. The king laughingly assented to Hugh's request, calling him a terrible fellow who had almost beggared him.

The promise that the king made to build them a chapel and a house was not fulfilled very quickly, with the consequence that the monks became angry, and one of them, a fierce Burgundian, announced that he would go to the king and speak plainly to him of his faults. Hugh accompanied him. The proud monk rebuked the king for not keeping his promises and warned him that he could not take his money with him, and indeed used a freedom of speech which lacked in the courtesy with which Hugh addressed the monarch when Henry appealed to him.

'What do you think, my good fellow,' said Henry, 'will you forsake me too?'

'My Lord,' said Hugh, 'I am less desperate than my brothers. You have much work upon your hands, and I can feel for you. When God shall please, you will have leisure to attend to us.'

'By my soul,' Henry answered, 'you are one that I will never part with while I live.'

When the see of Lincoln fell vacant, Henry commanded the prebends of the Cathedral, who were a wealthy and time-serving group, to elect Hugh as Bishop. They rather reluctantly obeyed him. But Hugh was not satisfied with an election which was the result of a Royal command, and sent the prebends back to pray that his election, if made, might have a higher authority than that of a secular monarch. They persisted, after prayer, in his election; but even then he would not accept the bishopric until he was commanded to do it by his monastic superior.

After he was consecrated Bishop, he fulfilled his duties as he understood them with simplicity and fearlessness; he even came into conflict with the King, who had really been kind to him, because he insisted on excommunicating his chief forester, and refused to give to a courtier a vacant prebend. The king commanded him to come to Woodstock, and prepared when he arrived to show him that he was seriously displeased.

'Then followed one of the most singular scenes in English history—a thing veritably true, which oaks still standing in Woodstock Park may have witnessed. As soon as word was brought that the Bishop was at the park gate, Henry mounted his horse, rode with his retinue into a glade in the forest, where he alighted, sat down upon the ground with his people, and in this position prepared to receive the criminal. The Bishop approached—no one rose or spoke. He saluted the king; there was no answer. Pausing for a moment, he approached, pushed aside gently an earl who was sitting at Henry's side, and himself took his place. Silence still continued.'

The silence was broken by a humorous reference of the Bishop, understood by no one present except the king, to some of the monarch's ancestors, which made the king literally shake with laughter.

After the king had given an explanation of his laughter, he said to the Bishop: 'My good sir, what do you mean by excommunicating my head forester, and when I make a small request of you, why is it that you not only do not come to see me, but do not send me so much as a civil answer?'

Hugh replied: 'I know myself to be indebted to your highness for my late promotion. I considered that your highness's soul would be in danger if I was found wanting in the discharge of my duties; . . . To wait on you on such a subject I thought superfluous, since your highness approves, as a matter of course, of whatever is rightly ordered in your realm.'

But perhaps even more remarkable were the Bishop's relations with Richard Cœur de Lion. Richard, after his return from captivity in Austria, was embroiled in war with the French king. Lacking money, he turned to the English Bishops to supply him. He demanded that each prelate should supply him with 300 knights at his own cost to serve in the war. The time-serving Archbishop Hubert and the Bishop of London responded to this demand; but at a Council of Bishops, Hugh of Lincoln declined to do so, because, though his diocese was legally obliged to supply military service for home defence, it was under no obligation to supply soldiers for foreign wars. He was supported in the Council by the Bishop of Salisbury and the Council ended in confusion.

The Archbishop informed the king that through the objections of the Bishop of Lincoln, it was impossible to obey his command. Richard, with all his noble qualities, when angry had the temper of a fiend. In his fury, he replied instantly with an order to seize and confiscate the property of the rebellious prelates; but as Hugh threatened to excommunicate anyone who carried out this order, the royal officers hesitated to act, knowing that he would keep his word. Though the prelates advised Hugh to give way, having already brought to his knees the Bishop of Salisbury, Hugh refused and resolved to go to France and meet the king himself. The king's anger was so great that some of his servants besought Hugh at least to send some conciliatory message before he faced the raging Lion. He took no notice of them, but went himself straight to the Cathedral of Roche d'Andeli where the king was hearing Mass. An extraordinary scene was enacted, which Froude describes in the following words:

' "Kiss me, my lord King," said the Bishop. It was the ordinary greeting between the sovereign and the spiritual peers. The king averted his face still further.

' "Kiss me, my Lord," said Hugo again, and he caught Cœur de Lion by the vest and shook him. Abbot Adam standing shivering behind.

' "*Non meruisti*—thou hast not deserved it," growled Richard.

' "I have deserved it," replied Hugh, and shook him harder.

'Had he shown fear, Cœur de Lion would probably have trampled on him, but who could resist such marvellous audacity? The kiss was given. The Bishop passed up to the altar and became absorbed in the service; Cœur de Lion curiously watching him.

'When Mass was over there was a formal audience, but the result of it was decided already. Hugh declared his loyalty in everything, save what touched his duty to God. The king yielded, and threw the blame of the quarrel on the too complaisant primate.

'Even this was not all. The Bishop afterwards requested a private interview. He told Richard solemnly that he was uneasy for his soul, and admonished him, if he had anything on his conscience to confess it.

'The king said he was conscious of no sin, save of a certain rage against his French enemies.

' "Obey God!" the Bishop said, "and God will humble your enemies for you—and you for your part take heed you offend not Him or hurt your neighbour. I speak in sadness, but rumour says you are unfaithful to your queen."

'The Lion was tamed for the moment. The king acknowledged nothing, but restrained his passion, only observing afterwards, "If all Bishops were like my lord of Lincoln, not a prince among us could lift his head against them".'

St Hugh seems to have had genuine affection for Henry and Richard, but for the treacherous John contempt. After the funeral of Richard I, Hugh met at Fontevrault the new King John, who made a profusion of promises to the Bishop of Lincoln as to his future conduct.

'I trust you mean what you say,' he said in reply, 'you know that I hate lying.'

John produced an amulet which he wore round his neck with a chain. That, he seemed to think, would help him to walk straight.

The bishop looked at it scornfully. 'Do you trust in a senseless stone?' he said. 'Trust in the living rock in heaven—the Lord Jesus Christ. Anchor your hope in Him and He will direct you.'[2]

St Hugh's scorn of John's amulet was typical of his feeling about charms and relics, so much relied upon by the men of his age. He had no credulous reverence even for alleged miracles. Abbot Adam, who says he saw him work many miracles, also tells us that he took no notice of them. His grim humour was shown by a remarkable incident. Once he visited a church, famous for its relics, and was shown a bone of St Mary Magdalen, after Mass had been said in preparation for its veneration. This precious relic was wrapped in a case, and within the case was wrapped in silk.

The bishop asked to look at the bone itself; and no one venturing to touch it, he borrowed a knife and calmly slit the covering. He took it up, whatever it may have been, gazed at it, raised it to his lips as if to kiss it, and then suddenly with a strong grip of his teeth bit a morsel out of its side. A shriek of sacrilege rang through the church. Looking round quietly the Bishop said: 'Just now we were handling in our unworthy fingers the body of the Holy One of all. We passed Him between our teeth and down into our stomach; why may we not do the like with the members of his saints?'

One incident regarded by the people of the time as illustrative of the miracle-working power of the Saint was that of the famous swan, always associated with the name of Hugh. The bird, says Adam, was as much larger than other swans as a swan is than a goose. It was a savage bird which frightened the people

[2] Froude, *A Bishop of the Twelfth Century*.

of the district. When Hugh at any time came back from his travels to his residence, the great swan came trumpeting up to meet him, put his beak into his pockets where were bread-crumbs, and followed him about like a dog. 'A miracle,' said the people. The mind of the time seems to have sought a super-natural explanation of any event that was slightly unusual, whereas the mind of our time seeks a natural explanation of all things, some of which are beyond nature. Hugh himself, though naturally a man of his times, suffered little from the credulity of his contemporaries. He disliked relic worship, and dis-approved of the people running to and fro to view wonders, so he said: 'Let unbelievers go rushing after signs and wonders. What have we to do with such things who partake every day of the heavenly sacrifice?'

St Hugh, as Bishop of Lincoln, was involved in the political as well as the ecclesiastical life of the country, but of that I have no space to write. His probity and justice were universally acknowledged. Though always an ascetic himself, neither eating flesh nor drinking wine, as Abbot Adam tells us, he was a good table companion. He did not make others victims of his own abstinences. He showed kindness to his assistant priests, and actually commanded delicate men, whose custom it was to receive communion fasting, to eat and trust in God.

Many times the dominance of his personality is shown, as when he quietened savage mobs unarmed. He was kindly and merciful to every sort of outcast. Once he protected a felon who was being driven to execution and appealed to the Bishop for help. Hugh faced the authorities and told them that where the Bishop was, the Church was. The Church was a sanctuary to anyone who fled to it, and thus he saved the felon from execution. It is probable of course, that there is more in this story than Adam reads.

One of the most remarkable things at his funeral was the presence of a hundred Jews, who at that time were treated with abominable cruelty, as the records of the reign of John show.

It must have been almost a unique event for Jews to attend a Christian funeral, and is a remarkable expression of the gratitude of unfortunate people to this great man.

He was pitiful to all needy, poor, and especially diseased people like the lepers. The lot of the victims of this terrible disease was one of indescribable misery. Everyone shunned them and regarded them as men under the curse of God. St Hugh not only pitied them, but built hospitals for them (he must have been one of the earliest men to have done it) which he visited himself. Of such visitations Abbot Adam gives the following vivid account:

> Pardon, blessed Jesus, the unhappy soul of him who tells this story! when I saw my master touch those bloated and livid faces; when I saw him kiss the bleared eyes or eyeless sockets, I shuddered with disgust. But Hugh said to me that these afflicted ones were flowers of Paradise, pearls in the coronet of the Eternal King waiting for the coming of their Lord, who in his own time would change their forlorn bodies into the likeness of his own glory.

Merciful, generous, and large minded as he was, Hugh of Lincoln very much disliked worldly and time-serving Bishops. In his intercourse with them, his tongue, as he himself says, could be more bitter than pepper. He had much controversy with the too-complacent Archbishop Hubert. When returning from his last journey to France, Hugh fell ill in London, and it became evident that he was not going to live.

The Archbishop visited him and when sitting by his bed, after the usual condolences, suggested that the Bishop of Lincoln might like to use the opportunity to repent of any sharp expressions which he had occasionally been betrayed into using. As the hint was not taken, he referred especially to himself as one of those who had something to complain of.

'Indeed, your grace,' replied Hugh, 'there have been passages of words between us and I have much to regret in relation to them. It is not, however, what I have said to your grace, but what I have omitted to say. I have more feared to offend your grace than to offend my Father in heaven. I have withheld words which I ought to have spoken, and I have thus sinned against your grace and desire your forgiveness. Should it please God to spare my life I purpose to amend that fault.'

The funeral of St Hugh was a demonstration of the respect and admiration of the English people, from the King on his throne to the outcast Jews, rarely paralleled in English history. Two kings, three Archbishops, fourteen bishops, a hundred abbots, and as many earls and barons waited on a hill, a mile from the town, to receive the sad procession.

This great man, whose memory should be treasured by all Englishmen, was indeed 'the shadow of a great rock in a weary land'.

By a remarkable coincidence, St Hugh's day, 17th November, was the day on which another Hugh, honoured in his time, Hugh Price Hughes, died. He too was a man of wise and cheerful boldness. The phrase he coined, 'Christian audacity', was his watchword, and typical of his actions both in the religious and political life of his century.

What is the secret of 'cheerful boldness' and 'Christian audacity'. In the Collect of the day we pray for grace not only to be bold, but to have just cause for boldness, even the fear and love of God alone.

The hymn we so often sing expresses the secret of the fearless-ness of Hugh of Lincoln:

> *Fear Him, ye saints, and you will then*
> *Have nothing else to fear.*

CHAPTER TWELVE

CITIZENSHIP WEEK

(23rd Sunday after Trinity [1954])

Epistle: Philippians 3¹⁷.   *Gospel:* Matthew 22¹⁵.

'Render therefore unto Cæsar the things which are Cæsar's; and unto God the things which are God's.'

'Ye are a colony of heaven.'

> *With songs to Zion we return,*
> *Contending for our native heaven.*

THE Methodist Conference instructs its people to observe the week beginning with the 3rd Sunday of November, as Citizenship Week. In 1954, by a happy coincidence, this was the date of the 23rd Sunday after Trinity, the teaching of the Gospel and Epistle of which may be said to be concentrated in the two quotations: 'Render therefore unto Cæsar the things that are Cæsar's . . .' and 'Ye are a colony of heaven'. The latter quotation seems to be a happier translation even than that of the Revised Version: 'Your citizenship is in heaven.' The special attention called for, on the 3rd Sunday of November, to the evils of intemperance may well be enforced by St Paul's words in the Epistle: 'Brethren, be followers together of me, and mark them which walk so as ye have us for an ensample. (For many walk, of whom I have told you often, and now tell you even weeping, that they are the enemies of the cross of Christ: whose end is destruction, whose God is their belly, and whose glory is in their shame, who mind earthly things.)' Intemperate action, the Apostle reminds them, is not possible for citizens of heaven. But it is of the general duties of the Christian citizen that I shall write.

Let it first be noted that the words of Jesus, 'Render therefore unto Cæsar the things that are Cæsar's', clearly define a secular department of life, which is to be served by secular methods as the Christian duty of His followers. St Paul in Romans 13 clearly explains our Lord's meaning: 'Let every soul be subject unto the higher powers. For there is no power but of God: the powers that be are ordained of God. Whosoever therefore resisteth the power, resisteth the ordinance of God.'

Methods of government of course change. What I wish to emphasize is the fact that secular duties are of Divine ordination. Thus one of the things we are rendering to God is our obedience to Cæsar in his own sphere. The clash of these two loyalties, so often to be observed in Christian history, arises from the failure to realize, on the one hand, that obedience to Cæsar is of Divine ordinance, and on the other, that though it is secondary, secular duties are compulsive on Christians.

There was no saying of our Lord's that irritated and infuriated the apostate Emperor Julian more than this. Henrik Ibsen's dialogue between Julian and the philosopher Maximus is a true picture of the Apostate's sentiment. When Maximus recommended Julian to return to the Galileans, the Emperor replied:

'You know well that that is impossible. Emperor and Galilean! How reconcile that contradiction? Yes, this Jesus Christ is the greatest rebel that ever lived. What was Brutus —what was Cassius, compared with him? They murdered only the man Julius Cæsar; but he murders all that is called Cæsar or Augustus. Is peace conceivable between the Galilean and the Emperor? Is there room for them both upon the earth? For he lives on the earth, Maximus—the Galilean lives, I say, however thoroughly both Jews and Romans imagined that they had killed him;—he lives in the rebellious minds of men; he lives in their scorn and defiance of all visible authority.

' "Render unto Cæsar the things that are Cæsar's—and to God the things that are God's!" Never has the mouth of man uttered a more crafty saying than that. What lies behind it? What, and how much, belongs to the Emperor? That saying is nothing but a bludgeon wherewith to strike the crown from off the Emperor's head.'

The Roman Emperor could tolerate no superior to himself. He was a god in his own right. Most of the Christians martyred under the Empire were men and women who refused to burn incense in acknowledgement of this claim.

During the Middle Ages nothing is more conspicuous than the clash between Church and Empire, the Church sometimes interfering with the secular rights of the Empire, and the Empire with the spiritual rights of the Church; the double loyalty issued in confusing misunderstanding. But is this the true issue? Is it not rather of an individual character? The voice of God is heard in the conscience of men, and the martyrs of all times have had to make the individual choice. We honour today Sir Thomas More, because he refused to acknowledge the sovereignty in the Church of a most unchristian monarch, and equally, I think, honour is due to Hugh Latymer, because he refused to recognize the authority of Queen Mary in matters of religion. In a way it is not untrue to say that Thomas More was the first Nonconformist martyr. He refused, as so many of them afterwards refused, to accept a religion dictated by the State. Conscience is the supreme voice of God.

We are privileged in our own country by the fact that conscience is recognized as higher than secular law courts. Whether one agrees or not with the pacifists, Great Britain has decided that where a man can be demonstrated to be sincere in the conviction that he should not take arms, he will not be forced to fight. That is to say, conscience is placed above the law.

I know no writing which expresses the double loyalty and the conflicts arising from it so effectively as the famous hymn of Spring-Rice:

> *I vow to thee, my country, all earthly things above,*
> *Entire and whole and perfect, the service of my love;*
> *The love that asks no question, the love that stands the test,*
> *That lays upon the altar the dearest and the best;*

The love that never falters, the love that pays the price,
The love that makes undaunted the final sacrifice.

And there's another country, I've heard of long ago,
Most dear to them that love her, most great to them that know;
We may not count her armies, we may not see her King;
Her fortress is a faithful heart, her pride is suffering;
And soul by soul and silently her shining bounds increase,
And her ways are ways of gentleness and all her paths are peace.

The devotion to his country—to the secular realm—is clearly defined as an earthly thing, to which the devotion to the other Country whose ways are ways of gentleness and all her paths are peace, is superior. Reasonable objection has often been made to the phrase, 'The love that asks no question'. The Nuremberg trials are quoted as evidence that patriotic love should ask questions. It would seem to me that Spring-Rice means to suggest that the highest loyalty is to God, to which even the patriotic love which asks no questions is ultimately subservient.

It is important to remember in a country like our own, a democratic country, that our modes of government are different from those of the Roman Empire. Indeed, we ourselves are not only subjects, but governors. We elect our own rulers, and to render to Cæsar the things that are Cæsar's is to take our part in the political life of the country, and, as citizens of heaven, never to forget the obligation to make the kingdoms of this world the Kingdom of our God and His Christ.

There is a certain pietism which rejects secular duty as worldly, because it fails to realize that secular obligations are definitely imposed by our Lord in such words as 'Render therefore unto Cæsar the things that are Cæsar's'. A great hymn of Charles Wesley's, said to have been in the eighteenth century the most popular of all his hymns, apparently puts a valuation on escapism which his followers today could not accept. I refer to the hymn, 'Leader of faithful souls and guide . . .'. Of course it is true to say:

We have no abiding city here,
But seek a city out of sight.

But it is only in a relative sense that we can sing: 'This earth, we know, is not our place.' Surely our place is where God puts us! But even if we are here only as lodgers, we cannot escape from a lodger's obligation.

I remember Mr Arthur Henderson, that great organizer of the Labour Party, telling me years ago that he met, when canvassing at an election, a lady who told him that she did not vote at elections because the only King she believed in was Jesus. He told her that she at least ought to use her lodger's vote. This seems to me a very fair putting of the situation. If we realize, as the Gospel surely teaches us, that Christ came to set up a kingdom on earth and that He Himself believed and enforced secular duties, we are not obeying our King unless we seek first His Kingdom here on earth.

There is much in this hymn that we do well to sing, so long as we remember that it is our duty to pray: 'Thy kingdom come on earth as it is in heaven.' Remembering this, we can still find inspiration in this hymn. We may sing:

> *With songs to Zion we return,*
> *Contending for our native heaven,*

and the songs of the home land will be inspiring; yet we must not only sing, but strive and contend to make a heaven on earth.

There are two lines of practical value omitted from the hymn, because John Wesley disliked the sentimental character of the first four lines of the stanza,

> *From Zion's top the breezes blow*
> *And cheer us in the vales below.*

St Paul's figure that we have our citizenship in Heaven, or that we are a colony of heaven, gives to us a key to the way in which we should render unto Cæsar the things that are Cæsar's. When our Lord went home to His Father He went to prepare a place for us. As long as we live on earth our duty is to prepare a place for Him. The Advent exhortation of John the Baptist is never out of date, 'Prepare ye the way of the Lord. Make his paths straight.'

The figure of a British Colony is in many ways helpful to an understanding of our secular duties. Our early colonists girdled the earth with little Englands. As they were not good linguists, they made their own language dominant in many parts of the earth. They preserved English customs and established English methods of government. They had twofold obligations, one to their country, and one to the new colony they were founding; but the thought of the old homeland was ever in their minds. They were primarily citizens of England, prizing their citizenship whilst developing new lands. Even in countries which now have become independent Dominions of self-governing people, the home instinct remains.

A few years ago when I visited Australia, I became acquainted with a family in which I was greatly interested. When I inquired about the children of the home, they told me that John was successful in his profession and Mary happily married, and then they said: 'But Thomas', and said it very quietly, 'he has gone home'. I felt I ought to condole with their loss, but was glad to think that they thought that he was in heaven, when suddenly I realized that 'going home' still meant to the people of the third generation of Australia going to England. Surely here we have a figure of the double loyalty of Christians—to the heavenly homeland and heavenly King, as well as to the new country they are forming.[1]

[1] Like most analogies, this one can be pressed too far. The quite noble conception today, that England is training the backward races in the science of self-government, is rather a new Colonial conception, and certainly cannot be used as an analogy of the double loyalty of Christians. To the Christian there never can be but one King. We do not live to train people to be independent of Jesus, but to acknowledge his Kingship. To do otherwise would be to inculcate the Communist ideal, which Arnold Toynbee has called, not inappropriately, an oriental Christian heresy. Christians have alas too often failed to practise their own Gospel, and the Communists, partly perhaps as a consequence, have tried to make a heaven on earth without believing in Heaven. However successful or unsuccessful their attempt to make a secularist paradise,

I remember reading a story of two travellers in a mountainous and largely undeveloped country. One of them, when walking, surprised the other by the bulkiness of the bundle he carried on his back. When they got to some place overnight, he found that the secret of the bundle was that the man had carried with him a barrel-organ. When overcome by loneliness, the man insisted on playing it, and since its resources were very limited, the result was the continued repetition of four familiar wheezy hymn-tunes. He did not play it for the sake of having a feast of music; it was just his cure for home-sickness. When he played 'At even, ere the sun was set', he pictured his native village, the familiar church, the running stream, the well-known faces; and when he played 'Tell me the old, old story', he looked through the window of a familiar cottage, and pictured his old father and mother reading the family Bible. Then tears sprang to his eyes, and the narrator of this story, a well-known littérateur, confessed the tears sprang to his eyes as well. In all the desolation of that country, dreams of homeland comforted the man and justified his barrel-organ.

Heaven is not only a goal, but an inspiration. The British Empire was built up out of nostalgia—homesickness for England. Homesickness for heaven can make the Kingdom of God on earth. If they had spent all their time with the barrel-organ, they would, of course, have failed in the civilizing work they really came to do. But there is much to be said for the barrel-organ, for the inspiration that comes from the thought of the homeland has encouraged the colonist many a time in his construction of the new country overseas. So we may say the equivalent for the citizens of heaven who are colonists on earth is the practise of worship of which hymn-singing is a conspicuous feature.

Sometimes thoughts of the heavenly city have been

its very secularism will bring about its ultimate failure. For our analogy, we need the old Colonial rule of loyalty to the country from which we come, —'our native heaven'—as well as service to the new community which is to be built up.

substituted for secular duty, but this does not seem to be a conspicuous danger of our own days. Nothing is of greater practical importance in the building of the City of God on earth, than the worship which gives to us visions of that City.

The Bible has many visions of the City of God; none to me are more entrancing than those of the prophet Zechariah, who pictured a city of peace, without fortifications, but surrounded by Jehovah Himself as a wall of fire, a city where old men lean on their staves and little children play in the street. The gates of it are to be opened not only to the Jews, but to all people. The King comes into it, not riding on a war horse, but on an ass, the symbol of peace. That vision of the City of God is one that every Christian should have in mind. It is to be achieved, not merely by song, though it is true that

> From Zion's top the breezes blow
> And cheer us in the vales below.

Work is needed, secular work, secular politics. It is not good enough to say, 'Politics are a dirty game'; the Christian is here to make them clean. Christian politics do not necessarily imply loyalty to a particular Party; but they *do* imply secular effort, the discharge of the duties that we all have to the secular State. In the great vision of the ideal City in the Book of Revelation, we are told that 'nought that defileth shall enter in'; and we are under obligation to fight against the defiling sins which so far have destroyed every civilization on earth. We have a work of cleansing to do; but more than that negative work, let us remember that we have to build love, for the King of the City is the 'King of Love', and those who inhabit it when it is set up on earth, are the family of God, ruled by the heavenly Father.

Worship gives us encouragement and help. We must never forget the heavenly city, our homeland; but when we seek the city still out of sight, it is a city descending to earth for which we seek. The homeland is not only the goal to which pilgrims travel, but the inspiration to all who seek first the Kingdom of God and His righteousness.